White P
MountainBiking
The Pure Trails

VERTEBRATE **PUBLISHING**

Design and production by Vertebrate Publishing, Sheffield
www.**v-publishing**.co.uk

White Peak
MountainBiking
The Pure Trails

Written by
Jon Barton

White Peak
MountainBiking
The Pure Trails

VG Copyright © 2014 **Vertebrate Graphics Ltd.**

VP Published by **Vertebrate Publishing.**
First published in 2006 by Vertebrate Graphics Ltd and reprinted in 2009.
This second edition first published in 2014 by Vertebrate Publishing,
an imprint of Vertebrate Graphics Ltd.

ISBN 978-1-910240-05-2

Front cover: Kim Russon on the Calver Circuit, near Hassop. Photo: Tim Russon.
Back cover: Singletrack above Coombs Dale on the Great Longstone ride. Photo: John Coefield.
Photography by John Coefield unless otherwise credited.

All maps reproduced by permission of Ordnance Survey
on behalf of The Controller of Her Majesty's Stationery Office.
© Crown Copyright. 100025218

Designed by Nathan Ryder. Produced by Rod Harrison.
www.**v-graphics**.co.uk
Printed in China.

MIX
Paper from
responsible sources
FSC® C016973

COMBI: 1, 9, 12

Contents

Introduction vii
Acknowledgements viii
How to Use this Book x
A Note on Trail Resurfacing xi
Rights of Way xii
The Bike xii
Essential Kit xiii
Night Riding xiv
General Safety xiv
In the Event of an Accident xv
Rules of the (Off) Road xv
Planning Your Ride xvi
Maps & Symbols xvi
White Peak Area Map
& Route Finder xviii

SECTION 1 – CLASSICS

Classics Introduction xx
1 ▲ The Quarry Trail – 10.5km 5
2 ▲ Shillito Woods – 14km 9
3 ▲ Ashover Singletrack – 13km 13
4 ▲ Dark & White – 13.75km 17
5 ▲ Grangemill – 17km 21
6 ▲ Bakewell Circuit – 17km 25
7 ▲ Middleton Circuit – 17.5km 29
8 ▲ Linacre North – 23km 33

SECTION 2 – ENDUROS

Enduros Introduction 38
9 ▲»▲ Calver Circuit – 20km 43
10 ▲»▲ Eastern Moors Tour – 20km ... 47
11 ▲»▲ Cheedale & the
         Wye Valley – 21.5km 53
12 ▲»▲ Great Longstone – 18km 59   GD WCT WIN 76
13 ▲»▲ Cromford Circuit – 21km 63
14 ▲»▲ Buxton & the
         Goyt Valley – 25+15km 69
15 ▲ Holymoorside – 21km 75
16 ▲ Bakewell Slice – 25km 81
17 ▲»▲ Manifold Valley – 24.5km 87
18 ▲ Gradbach – 26km 91
19 ▲»▲ South Buxton
         Circuit – 15/26km 97

SECTION 3 – EPICS

Epics Introduction 102
20 ▲ Macclesfield Forest
      Classic – 23km 107
21 ▲ Five Dales Circuit – 36km 113
22 ▲ Linacre Classic – 35km 119
23 ▲»▲ Hope Valley Circuit – 45km . 125
24 ▲ Rowsley Circuit – 38.5km 131

SECTION 4 – BONUS SECTION

Bonus Section Introduction 136
Hollinsclough Descents 140
The Pennine Bridleway 143
Family Rides 144
Top Ten Downhills 148
Top Ten Climbs 150
Top Ten Singletracks 152

APPENDIX 154

ROUTE GRADES
▲ = EASY ▲ = MEDIUM ▲ = HARD (see page xi)

LIMESTONE, CHARACTERISTIC OF THE WHITE PEAK

Introduction

It would be a real shame if the White Peak, an area so full of potential, of deep valleys, high limestone hills and thick, leafy woodland, were not also full of legal trails. Happily enough, it's laced with them. Not only that, but they're some of the best trails in the country, the sort that leave you wondering 'who built this, and if it were not specifically for mountain biking, then why?'

Whether you like to ride smoothly and delicately, flitting through the trees and over roots, or in a less subtle manner, being knocked sideways by a big block of limestone whilst pinballing downhill at mach 39, there is a contender for your personal favourite piece of trail in the White Peak (I know everyone says this, but it's true, honestly!).

Although less well known than the more barren Dark Peak, the White Peak boasts some tremendous riding and, for some, its relatively unspoilt aspect is of great appeal. This guide complements its companion, *Peak District Mountain Biking – Dark Peak Trails*, describing all of the excellent biking in the southern half of the Peak District National Park, and also providing a little reminder of what's further north, in gritstone land.

The routes cover not only the limestone plateaux and dales, but all the idiosyncrasies of the area as well: the upper reaches of the River Dove and its rocky byways, the intricate singletrack traversing the open moorland of the Eastern Edges, and the magnificent vista of the River Wye, as it carves its way through the beds of limestone. It ventures upon the industrial relics of the Peak – the abandoned railway lines, viaducts, disused (and active) quarries, mines and waterways.

This new edition features four new routes, numerous tweaked routes and untouched classic routes. And of course the now standard OS maps. Indeed, researching, re-riding and re-writing this second edition has been very rewarding; a fine reminder of the wonderful landscape, wildlife and mountain bike action in the White Peak. Enjoy.

Jon Barton

Acknowledgements

A big 'Thank You!' to all my riding companions over the years. In particular, thanks to everyone who has helped in compiling this book. Andy Heading has been a great inspiration, not only a superb snapper for the first edition but a great source of route info, local knowledge and general support. Thanks also to the hard working team at Vertebrate for their second-to-none efforts in production; John Coefield for his Herculean work compiling and editing this second edition – John and Tom Fenton also wrote most of the new content, Nathan Ryder and Rod Harrison for their excellent design skills and Tom Fenton for being editor-in-chief for the first edition. Thanks also to Nick Cotton for his excellent *Traffic Free Cycling* book, the inspiration for our Family Rides section, and to Rachel Bennett and Danny Udall from the Eastern Moors Partnership for their help with the new Eastern Moors route. Thanks to John Coefield and Tim Russon for their great photography, and to the photographic models: John Horscroft, Tom Fenton, Richard Barson and Tim and Kim Russon. And, finally, thanks to Gráinne and of course Thomas James.

ASHOVER SINGLETRACK

PEAK BIKE CODE

PROTECT
THE TRAIL
KEEP SINGLETRACK SINGLE!

ENJOY
YOUR RIDE
THE PEAK IS FOR EVERYONE!

ABIDE
BY THE COUNTRYSIDE CODE
LEAVE NO TRACE, LEAVE GATES AS YOU FIND THEM, PROTECT THE ENVIRONMENT!

KEEP
SMILING!
ALWAYS GIVE WAY, CHAT TO EVERYONE!

RIDE SHEFFIELD
WWW.RIDESHEFFIELD.ORG.UK

WWW.V-PUBLISHING.CO.UK

WWW.EASTERNMOORS.ORG.UK

How to Use This Book

Riding in the White Peak

This book should provide you with all of the information that you need for an enjoyable, trouble-free and successful ride in the White Peak area of the Peak District. There are rides on the Peak's eastern fringe, on the singletrack of Linacre near Chesterfield, bigger White Peak tours around Bakewell, Rowsley and Chatsworth, honorary Dark Peak rides against the western edge of the Peak near Macclesfield Forest, and actual Dark Peak rides up towards the upper edge of the White Peak and the Hope Valley. There's great variety – in trail surface, difficulty (both up and down), scenery and length. Something for everyone.

As with the riding in most of the UK, it's worth bearing a few things in mind for some of the rides (these are things we've generally pointed out in the individual routes):

Some of the rides, such as those around Linacre, Holymoorside, Cheedale and Bakewell are definitely best attempted in **dry weather** – or rather not after prolonged wet weather – as they can get rather muddy. Not only will they be not much fun to ride, but those precious strips of singletrack will get wider and wider, and nobody wants that.

The Linacre area rides can also get very **overgrown**, painfully so, from midsummer onwards. So they're definitely better suited to spring, early summer or autumn days.

In terms of **all-weather riding** in these parts, the Macc Forest stuff is your best bet, as it's predominantly on well surfaced forest trails and rocky trails. The new ride which takes in the concessionary bridleway along the top of Curbar and Froggatt edges also holds up fairly well, although we'd miss out the Totley Moor section.

The Routes

This guide contains 24 of the best routes in the southern half of the Peak District, with a few Dark Peak routes thrown in for good measure. Some of the rides are just as good in reverse and many get better on the second and third ride as you learn the best bits.

Classics are fairly short (but not necessarily easy), **Epics** are a little longer and require that bit more effort and **Enduros** step things up again.

Grades

Routes, climbs and descents are graded blue, red and black, in a similar system to that used at trail centres around the UK.

▲ = Easy   ▲ = Medium   ▲ = Hard

The grades are based on average conditions – good weather and not too wet and muddy. In a drought the routes will feel easier, in the depths of winter, harder. Grades consider technicality, length, climbs, navigation, and remoteness – so one 'black' route might be a short all-out technical test while another could be a big endurance challenge with tricky navigation. As ever, these grades are subjective. How you find a particular route, downhill or climb will be dictated by your own levels of fitness and skill.

Directions & Accuracy

While every effort has been made to ensure accuracy within the directions in this guide, things change and we are unable to guarantee that every detail will be correct. Please treat stated distances as guidelines. **Please exercise caution if a direction appears at odds with the route on the ground. A comparison between direction and map should see you on the right track.**

A Note on Trail Resurfacing

At the time of writing, some of the classic natural trails in the White Peak have been the victim of rather heavy-handed Right of Way maintenance and resurfacing work, primarily at the hands of Derbyshire County Council. Unfortunately, appeals to the authority for greater consideration of the beauty of the natural trail surface, safety issues and trail user conflicts, and general common sense have fallen on deaf ears. As a result, wonderful limestone features such as Wigley Lane near Rowland have been buried beneath a layer of ghastly, reclaimed tarmac scrapings. Wigley Lane isn't the only victim in the area, and that area around Great Longstone has suffered in particular.

The upshot of this is that we can't vouch that the trail as described in this guidebook will resemble the trail on the ground (see *Directions & Accuracy*). And while a rougher, technical surface would force a mountain biker to ride more slowly, on a smoother surface a cyclist will naturally be faster, so please be especially considerate of other trail users. Hopefully, in time, the local authorities will learn that they cannot simply ignore the interests of large user groups such as mountain bikers. Indeed they should embrace the input and enthusiasm of such groups.

Rights of Way

Countryside access in the UK hasn't been particularly kind to cyclists, although things are improving. We have 'right of way' on bridleways (blue arrows on signs) and byways (red arrows). However, having 'right of way' doesn't actually mean having the right of way, just that we're allowed to ride there – so give way to walkers and horse riders. We're also allowed to ride on green lanes and some unclassified roads, although the only way to determine which are legal and which aren't is to check with the local countryside authority. Obviously, cycle routes are also in.

Everything else is out of bounds (unless, of course, the landowner says otherwise). Riding illegally can upset walkers (who have every right to enjoy their day) and is, in many cases, technically classed as trespass (meaning you could be prosecuted for any damage caused). Not all tracks are signed, so it's not always obvious whether that great-looking trail you want to follow is an illegal footpath or a legal bridleway. That's why it's a good idea to carry a map with you on every ride.

The Bike

Any half-decent mountain bike will be fine (try and avoid a '£99 special'). A full suspension bike will add comfort and control. A lightweight race number will make hills easier and something with a bit of travel will help on technical descents. We'd pick a compromise somewhere between the three, depending on your personal preferences, although a lightweight 29er would be ideally suited to much of the riding in the White Peak.

Check everything's working – you won't be going uphill fast if your gears seize but equally you'll be a little quicker than planned if your brakes fail coming down. Pump the tyres up, check nothing's about to wear through and make sure that everything that should be tight is tight.

Essential Kit

Helmet

'The best helmet is the one that you're wearing.' Make sure it fits, you're wearing it correctly and that it won't move in a crash.

Clothing

You need to get your clothing right if you want to stay comfortable on a bike, especially in bad weather. The easiest way to do this is to follow a layering system. Begin with clothing made from 'technical' synthetic or wool fabrics that will wick the sweat away from your body and then dry quickly, keeping you dry and warm. Stay away from cotton – it absorbs moisture and holds onto it. If it's chilly, an insulating layer will keep you warm, and a wind/waterproof layer on the outside protects from the elements. Layers can then be removed or added to suit the conditions. Padded shorts are more comfortable, but the amount of Lycra on display is down to you. Baggy shorts, full-length tights and trousers are all available to match the conditions. Set off a little on the cold side – you'll soon warm up. Don't leave the warm clothes behind though, as the weather can turn quickly.

Gloves

Gloves ward off blisters and numb hands and help keep your fingers warm. They also provide a surprising amount of protection when you come off.

Footwear

Flat pedals/clipless – it's your call. Make sure you can walk in the shoes and that they have sufficient tread for you to do so. Consider overshoes if it's chilly.

Other essentials

As mentioned, take any necessary spares, tools, tube and pump, spare clothes, first aid kit, food and water. Stop short of the kitchen sink, as you'll still want to be able to actually ride your bike.

You'll need something to carry this lot in. We'd suggest a hydration pack, as they allow you to drink on the move and keep excess weight off the bike.

Maps

The Peak District is covered by the following **OS maps**, definitely worth the investment:
Ordnance Survey Explorer OL24 (1:25,000) The Peak District – White Peak Area
Ordnance Survey Explorer OL1 (1:25,000) The Peak District – Dark Peak Area
Ordnance Survey Landranger 119 (1:50,000) Buxton & Matlock

Night Riding

Night riding is ace! It's possible to enjoy an after-work ride in the depths of winter in your favourite off-road playground. But it's a completely different ball game and (hardly surprisingly) there are a few risks to be aware of.

Lights and batteries

Invest carefully in a lighting system. Consider battery life, weight, number/type of bulbs and power. Fully charge your battery before a ride (sounds like common sense, until you forget). Carry a secondary light source (such as a head torch) for emergencies (it's surprising what you can ride with a commuter light if you have to, although it isn't much fun). Pack a rear light for road sections and keep it clean.

Route planning and safety

Choose your ride on the basis of battery life. Time it yourself, don't necessarily rely on the manufacturer's information. Allow extra time – you'll be slower in the dark. Stay on ground that you are familiar with at first (night-time navigation in unfamiliar territory demands military expertise) and not too far from home. Ride with a friend. Watch out for the werewolves. Tell someone you're out. Ride within your limits – trees loom up very quickly in the dark!

General Safety

The ability to read a map, navigate in poor visibility and to understand weather warnings is essential. Don't head out in bad weather, unless you're confident and capable of doing so.

Some of the routes described point you at tough climbs and steep descents that can potentially be very dangerous. Too much exuberance on a steep descent in the middle of nowhere and you could be in more than a spot of bother, especially if you're alone. Consider your limitations and relative fragility.

Be self-sufficient. Carry food and water, spares, a tube and a pump. Consider a first-aid kit. Even if it's warm, the weather could turn, so take a wind/waterproof. Think about what could happen on an enforced stop. Pack lights if you could finish in the dark.

If you're riding solo, think about the seriousness of an accident – you might be without help for a very long time. Tell someone where you're going, when you'll be back and tell them once you are back. Take a mobile phone if you have one, but don't expect a signal. And don't call out the ambulance because you've grazed your knee.

Riding in a group is safer (ambitious overtaking manoeuvres excepted) and often more fun, but don't leave slower riders too far behind and give them a minute for a breather when they've caught up. Allow extra time for a group ride, as you'll inevitably stop and chat. You might need an extra top if you're standing around for a while. Ride within your ability, make sure you can slow down fast and give way to other users. Bells might be annoying, but they work. If you can't bring yourself to bolt one on, a polite 'excuse me' should be fine. On hot, sunny days, slap on some Factor 30+ and ALWAYS WEAR YOUR HELMET!

In the Event of an Accident
In the event of an accident requiring immediate assistance: Dial 999 and ask for POLICE or AMBULANCE. If you can supply the services with a grid reference of exactly where you are it should help to speed up their response time.

Mountain Rescue by SMS text
Another option in the UK is contacting the emergency services by SMS text – useful if you have a low battery or intermittent signal, but you do need to register your phone first. To register, simply text 'register' to 999 and then follow the instructions in the reply. Do it now – it could save yours or someone else's life. **www.emergencysms.org.uk**

Rules of the (Off) Road
1. Always ride on legal trails.
2. Ride considerately – give way to horses and pedestrians.
3. Don't spook animals.
4. Ride in control – you don't know who's around the next corner.
5. Leave gates as you find them – if you're unsure, shut them.
6. Keep the noise down and don't swear loudly when you fall off in front of walkers.
7. Leave no trace – take home everything you took out.
8. Keep water sources clean – don't take toilet stops near streams.
9. Enjoy the countryside and respect its life and work.

Planning Your Ride

1. Consider the ability/experience of each rider in your group. Check the weather forecast. How much time do you have available? Now choose your route.
2. Study the route description before setting off, and cross-reference it with the relevant map.
3. Bear in mind everything we've suggested about safety, clothing, spares and food and drink.
4. Get out there and get dirty.

Maps & Symbols

Ordnance Survey maps are the most commonly used, are easy to read and many people are happy using them. If you're not familiar with OS maps and are unsure of what the symbols mean, you can download a free map legend from **www.ordnancesurvey.co.uk**

We've included details of the relevant OS map for each route. To find out more about OS maps or to order maps please visit **www.ordnancesurvey.co.uk**

Here's a guide to the symbols and abbreviations we use on the maps and in our directions:

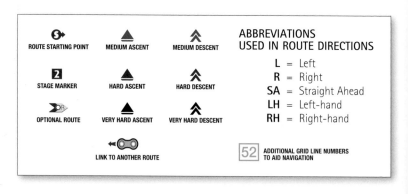

ROUTE STARTING POINT

STAGE MARKER

OPTIONAL ROUTE

LINK TO ANOTHER ROUTE

MEDIUM ASCENT

HARD ASCENT

VERY HARD ASCENT

MEDIUM DESCENT

HARD DESCENT

VERY HARD DESCENT

ABBREVIATIONS USED IN ROUTE DIRECTIONS

L = Left
R = Right
SA = Straight Ahead
LH = Left-hand
RH = Right-hand

52 **ADDITIONAL GRID LINE NUMBERS TO AID NAVIGATION**

DESCENT TO TENTERHILL

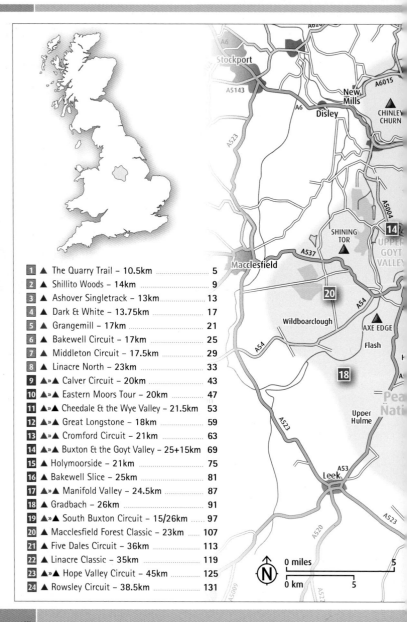

1	▲	The Quarry Trail – 10.5km	5
2	▲	Shillito Woods – 14km	9
3	▲	Ashover Singletrack – 13km	13
4	▲	Dark & White – 13.75km	17
5	▲	Grangemill – 17km	21
6	▲	Bakewell Circuit – 17km	25
7	▲	Middleton Circuit – 17.5km	29
8	▲	Linacre North – 23km	33
9	▲»▲	Calver Circuit – 20km	43
10	▲»▲	Eastern Moors Tour – 20km	47
11	▲»▲	Cheedale & the Wye Valley – 21.5km	53
12	▲»▲	Great Longstone – 18km	59
13	▲»▲	Cromford Circuit – 21km	63
14	▲»▲	Buxton & the Goyt Valley – 25+15km	69
15	▲	Holymoorside – 21km	75
16	▲	Bakewell Slice – 25km	81
17	▲»▲	Manifold Valley – 24.5km	87
18	▲	Gradbach – 26km	91
19	▲»▲	South Buxton Circuit – 15/26km	97
20	▲	Macclesfield Forest Classic – 23km	107
21	▲	Five Dales Circuit – 36km	113
22	▲	Linacre Classic – 35km	119
23	▲»▲	Hope Valley Circuit – 45km	125
24	▲	Rowsley Circuit – 38.5km	131

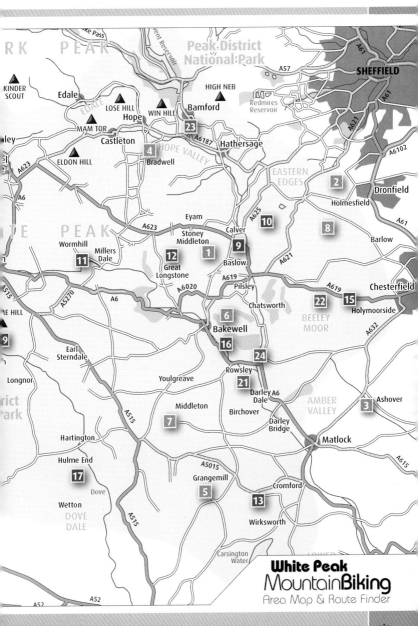

SECTION 1

Classics

A quick blast after work, a night loop you can finish before your lights run out, or a ride to squeeze in when you're short of time and energy. That's a classic. Relatively low on distance and never taking you too far from home, these are still good, solid rides – kind of like Fawlty Towers – highly entertaining, but not running for too long.

LONG DALE, ON THE MIDDLETON CIRCUIT

DESCENT TO MIDDLETON DALE

01 The Quarry Trail

Introduction

The Peak District National Park is a very busy place; there is a balancing act between tourists, recreational users, agriculture and industry. This short ride gives a flavour of everything that the White Peak stands for. Essentially a circuit of several huge quarries, it also takes in the plague village of Eyam, with its doilied tea rooms, the rough and tumble of proper mountain biking on the high farming pastures of Middleton Moor, and of course mineral and limestone workings galore. This route is ideal as an introduction to mountain biking and a great night ride.

The Ride

Starting from the large lay-by-cum-car park at the western end of Stoney Middleton, just opposite the Lovers Leap Garage, the ride heads down the dale, before traversing the Longstone Edge ridge, following a vein of fluorspar. The route then briefly leaves the quarry-scape behind, crossing the delightful Coombs Dale. It climbs back up then descends fast back to Stoney Dale before a final loop around Eyam drops you rapidly back to Stoney Middleton.

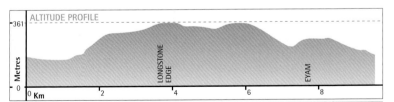

ALTITUDE PROFILE

361

Metres

0

0 Km   2   4   6   8

LONGSTONE EDGE

EYAM

THE QUARRY TRAIL   GRADE: ▲

TOTAL DISTANCE: 10.5KM » **TOTAL ASCENT**: 355M » **TIME**: 1–2 HRS » **START/FINISH**: STONEY MIDDLETON
START GRID REF: SK 227757 » **SATNAV**: S32 4TF » **PARKING**: LAY-BY ON A623, 50M EAST OF LOVERS LEAP GARAGE
OS MAP: EXPLORER OL24 THE PEAK DISTRICT – WHITE PEAK AREA » **PUB**: THE MOON, STONEY MIDDLETON TEL: 01433 630 203
CAFÉ: PEAK PANTRY, EYAM TEL: 01433 631 293.

Directions – The Quarry Trail

➊ Turn **R** out of the lay-by and ride downhill on the A623 through the village of Stoney Middleton. Turn **R** at the traffic lights at Calver crossroads. After about 500m, just after a lane joins on the left, turn **R** through a gate onto a track.

2 The track zigzags up, and up and up, eventually levelling out. Keep **L** at a vague fork, on the main track. Continue on to a track junction and turn **R**, keeping to the good track (ignore the tracks leading left and watch out for the big hole on your left). Keep **SA** on the main track for about 1.5km, until a bridleway joins from the right – take this. (If you start climbing past a big open quarry on your right, you've gone too far.)

3 Fun descent on stone and grass singletrack to Black Harry Gate. Bear **R** at the bottom to join the wide track and go **SA** up the steep, narrow climb opposite. Continue **SA** over the brow, **SA** across the lane and onto a descent past yet more quarries. Towards the bottom, heed the *Footpath/Bridleway* signs though the quarry and emerge, brakes permitting, slowly on to the busy A623.

4 Go **SA** across the main road and up the minor road to Eyam. In the village, take the first **R**, Lydgate, and follow this to where the tarmac path forks either side of a row of houses. Fork **L** onto a fast, sweeping descent, through a few gates. Meets tarmac at a gate near houses and drops into the maze of back streets of Stoney. Follow your nose back to the main road and turn **R** back up to the lay-by.

⛓ Making a day of it

Roll down the road to Calver (GR SK 239748) and pick up the Calver Circuit (see page 43). Follow it in reverse until you meet the Great Longstone ride (see page 59) near Rowland (GR SK 213721). Reverse this and return to The Quarry Trail at Black Harry Gate (GR SK 206743).

01 THE QUARRY TRAIL

SHILLITO WOODS SINGLETRACK

Introduction

A fantastic little ride that features a bucket-load of singletrack, a tough climb and one of the best trails in the White Peak. One of our favourite short rides, it makes a brilliant after-work blast or night ride. It's even easy to extend north or south if you find yourself wanting more.

There is a catch, however. Finding this ride at its best is tricky. If it's been wet recently, it'll be hard going. If it's the height of summer, it could be overgrown. And if the horse riders are out, you'll be doing a lot of stopping and starting. But get it right, in the spring when the trails are hard, fast and clear, and the route is a corker.

The Ride

It's only a couple of hundred metres before you're off road and on singletrack. The first run, down into Shillito Woods, is a fast and pedally affair that gets a touch trickier in the trees, with an awkward stream crossing towards the end. The second singletrack, reached after a couple of decent climbs, is pretty straightforward with some fun corners and a nice little drop that might catch out the unwary. Next, a lane climb leads to the highlight – Cartledge Lane. Starting fast and wide, it narrows to smooth singletrack that twists and turns gently downhill through trees. It's fantastic, only spoilt by the fact that the corners are a touch blind and there's always the worry that there'll be a horse just around the next one – so watch out! It's uphill from now on – literally. There's another singletrack descent you can throw in for fun, but otherwise it's straight up Johnnygate Lane. Steep at the beginning and rutted higher up, this is a tough test of both legs and skills – but well worth it for the singletrack earlier in the ride.

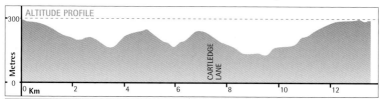

ALTITUDE PROFILE

CARTLEDGE LANE

Metres

0 Km 2 4 6 8 10 12

SHILLITO WOODS **GRADE:** ▲

TOTAL DISTANCE: 14KM » **TOTAL ASCENT**: 320M » **TIME**: 1.5-2.5 HRS » **START/FINISH**: CAR PARK NEAR SHILLITO WOODS **START GRID REF**: SK 295750 » **SATNAV**: N/A » **PARKING**: FREE CAR PARK » **OS MAP**: EXPLORER OL24 THE PEAK DISTRICT – WHITE PEAK AREA » **PUB**: NONE » **CAFÉ**: IT'S ONLY SHORT. TAKE A BANANA.

Directions – Shillito Woods

➊ Turn **L** out of the car park and on to the lane. After a couple of hundred metres, opposite the road junction, turn **R** through a gate onto a signed bridleway. Follow the wide track for approx. 100m and then bear slightly **R** onto narrower grassy singletrack. This runs straight ahead, become faster as it drops in to the trees. Jerk awkwardly across the stream and climb to a gate. Turn **R** onto a wide and well-surfaced track (formerly a nice little descent – hopefully it'll roughen up again in the future). This leads steeply uphill onto a narrow lane.

2 At the T-junction, turn **L** and speed downhill. Keep carefully **SA** at the junction and then, after approx. 100m, turn **L** onto a signed gravel bridleway. Climb this to the top and then follow the drive out to the lane.

3 **Easy to miss**: Turn **R** and climb the lane for around 800m before turning **R** onto a 'hidden' (but signed) bridleway tucked away between the entrance to a house and a stone wall. Speed down this, watching out for a) horses (!) and b) the drop and the gate halfway down. At the bottom, pop out onto the road and turn **L**.

4 It's a bit of a slog back up the road, but it's worth it. After 1km, turn **R** onto a lane as the road bends left – there's a bridleway sign on the far corner of the junction. Follow this lane until it ends (it's only a short way) and then continue **SA** onto the highlight of the ride. This starts as a wide track, but soon narrows into smooth singletrack that twists and turns its way gently downhill through trees. Watch out for horses.

5 At the bottom, continue **SA** to the T-junction with the road and turn **R**. At the crossroads, go **SA** and follow the lane to the end.

> For a little extra fun, there's a cracking little descent off to the **R** just before the dirt starts – go through the farm for a narrow and splashy downhill. Join the lane and then turn **R** on the main road to loop back to the crossroads.

6 Continue **SA** as the tarmac ends. This is a tough climb, but it's all rideable and is a nice challenge for the legs and skills. At the top, turn **R** at the road junction and follow the lane. Just before you arrive at the junction opposite the gate at the start of the ride turn **R** through the woods back to the car park.

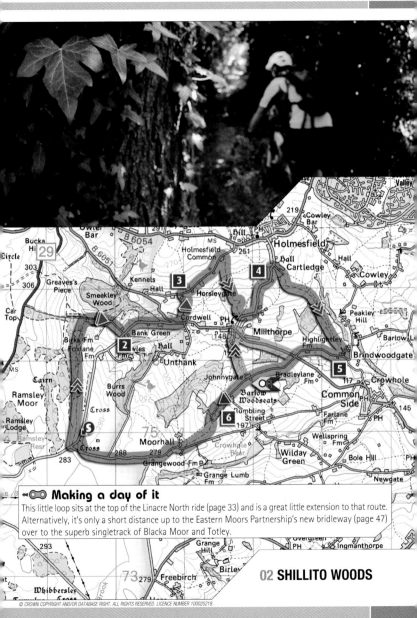

◄●◯◯ Making a day of it

This little loop sits at the top of the Linacre North ride (page 33) and is a great little extension to that route. Alternatively, it's only a short distance up to the Eastern Moors Partnership's new bridleway (page 47) over to the superb singletrack of Blacka Moor and Totley.

02 SHILLITO WOODS

03 Ashover Singletrack

13km

Introduction

Ashover is a funny old place for the mountain biker, being home to really rather excellent riding on an island of bridleways adrift in a sea of footpaths. The trick is finding the best way to link them up while avoiding the murderous A632. We don't claim to have solved the puzzle, but this is a fantastic ride, mainly on singletrack, with some good descents and one of the hardest climbs in this guide.

Although short, it's a test of your skills, with technical river crossings, the odd obstacle and sustained ups and downs. Oddly enough it makes an ideal test track for a new bike or bit of kit as it has a bit of everything, but is not too far to push home should the kit not live up to expectations, or if you want to ride bits again after tweaking shock pressures and the like. As is the case with much of the White Peak, the best times to ride this route are late spring or autumn when it is dry, and the vegetation is either yet to grow or is dying back.

The Ride

Tracing a loop around the Amber Valley, starting from the village of Ashover, this ride crosses the river, nips down a short descent and then kicks straight in with a big, and hard, climb. This is the toughest on the ride and if you can clean it, you're going well. The reward is a fantastic singletrack descent through a tunnel of trees. Fast and flowing, it's a real gem. Looping back round and up the hill once more, another tough climb leads up through a quarry. More technical than the first, it's shorter and less steep, making it a fun challenge which winches the rider to quiet lanes on the lip of the Amber Valley. Cross the A632 (yikes) before another great descent – one of the best in the area – and a final bit of trail lead back to Ashover.

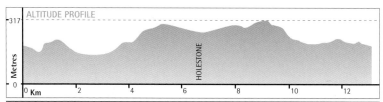

ALTITUDE PROFILE

Metres / 317 / 0

HOLESTONE

Km 0 2 4 6 8 10 12

ASHOVER SINGLETRACK　　　　　　　　　　　　**GRADE:** ▲

TOTAL DISTANCE: 13KM » **TOTAL ASCENT**: 380M » **TIME**: 1–2.5 HRS » **START/FINISH**: ASHOVER VILLAGE
START GRID REF: SK 349631 » **SATNAV**: S45 0AB » **PARKING**: ON-STREET PARKING IN ASHOVER VILLAGE
OS MAP: LANDRANDER 119 BUXTON & MATLOCK » **PUB**: OLD POETS' CORNER, ASHOVER TEL: 01246 590 888
CAFÉ: SANDWICH TIME.

Directions – Ashover Singletrack

➔ Head downhill from the parking, past the church towards the T-junction. Turn **L** and take the bridleway **R**, down the side of the Old Poets' Corner pub. Descend to the river, and then dig deep for a very tough climb – thankfully short lived. After the climb, the bridleway meets a track. Turn **L** along this and keep **SA**, ignoring the wide track to the right and the track down through the gateposts on the left (you're coming back up here in a minute). Climb and then descend superb narrow singletrack for approx. 1km and meet tarmac.

2 Continue **SA** down the lane, keeping left, and pass in front of the pub, turning **L** at the junction onto the road. Follow this towards Fallgate and after 300m turn **L** over a stone bridge signed *Jetting Street* and *Public Bridleway*. Follow this around to the right, through a gate onto a broad track climbing the hillside (don't drop to the riverside bridleway). After 1km meet your track from earlier and continue **SA** on the wide track to a T-junction.

3 Go **SA** onto a bridleway (stone slab surface) and head off up into the woods. Pleasant climbing emerges at old quarry workings. (Have a play on the tracks if you fancy.) Keep **SA** uphill, ignore the left fork heading down, and a final steep push gains tarmac and the road.

4 **SA** at this crossroads and after 75m turn **R** on Allen Lane. Follow this **SA**, taking the first **R**, past South Carolina Cottages, onto Whitelea Lane. Keep **SA** onto Lant Lane and meet the busy A632. Turn **R** and then first **L**. Head along this road and take the first **R** after 750m. Pass a car park and then take the farm track signed to Vernon Lane Farm.

5 Descend towards the farm before forking **L** at the gates, and follow this fantastic technical descent to the river. Ford it (at your peril!) or use the bridge. The second ford is a little less deep; follow the trail into the hamlet of Kelstedge. At the main road turn **L**, uphill, and after the last house (farm) take the broad track **R**. This soon improves into more singletrack and drops with interest back to the road. Turn **R** at the T-junction back into Ashover.

⊷⊙ Making a day of it
Why not make a 'night' of it instead? This isn't a bad little route to do in the dark – with lights, of course.

Northedge

03 ASHOVER SINGLETRACK

KIM RUSSON DESCENDING BRADWELL EDGE PHOTO: TIM RUSSON

04 Dark & White

Introduction

This is a full-on mountain bike route, sampling typical white and dark terrain, with challenging climbs and descents on both gritstone and limestone. Although the route has fine views, you won't notice them, as you will be pedalling hard on the climbs, or hanging in on the descents.

The Ride

From the Peak mountain bike capital of Hope, this route heads up Edale, before climbing the rocky lane onto the side of Win Hill known as Hope Brink. A fantastic descent speeds down to the hamlet of Aston, and then across the valley floor to Brough. Well warmed up, fit and skilful cyclists will style the steep climb of Brough Lane before descending to Bradwell. With a steady cooling-down past the cement works you'll make it back to Hope in time for tea.

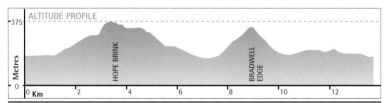

ALTITUDE PROFILE

HOPE BRINK

BRADWELL EDGE

Metres

0 Km 2 4 6 8 10 12

DARK & WHITE   GRADE: ▲

TOTAL DISTANCE: 13.75KM » **TOTAL ASCENT**: 530M » **TIME**: 1–2.5 HRS » **START/FINISH**: HOPE » **START GRID REF**: SK 171834 **SATNAV**: S33 6RD » **PARKING**: PAY AND DISPLAY, HOPE VILLAGE » **OS MAP**: EXPLORER OL1 THE PEAK DISTRICT – DARK PEAK AREA » **PUB**: PLENTY TO CHOOSE FROM IN HOPE » **CAFÉ**: WOODBINE CAFÉ, HOPE TEL: 07778 113 882.

❻ From the pay and display car park on the main road in Hope, leave the car park, turning **R**, and take the first **L** onto Edale Road, signposted *Edale*. Follow this road for just over 1km, before turning **R** (effectively **SA**) up Fullwood Stile Lane, just after crossing the river by the bridge on the bend. Up the lane, swing **L** at the top and steadily climb on worsening tarmac to a gate.

2 **SA** up the rocky lane, all very rideable for the determined. It soon levels off. Splash through the puddles, and a final sharp climb leads up to a junction by the gate. Turn back **R** (don't go through the gate) and follow the trail uphill, looking out for a small cairn after 750m, (if you reach another gate you have overshot). Fork **R** at the cairn, heading downhill on the fine trail.

3 Continue through a couple of gates, bearing **R** across the grassy field, heading for the muddy lane at the left side of the woods. Down the lane, through a couple of gates to reach tarmac at Edge Farm. Downhill to the junction. Turn **L** and at the summit of the second dip, turn **R** downhill on good fast tarmac, to soon reach the main road.

4 Turn **L** to the traffic lights, then **R** onto Brough Lane End. Cross the bridge and turn **L** up Brough Lane. Follow steepening tarmac up and then round to the **R**, uphill to where it becomes a steep lane (recently resurfaced). Persevere, as it eases once around the shallow rightward bend, where steady climbing leads up to a signed bridleway through a gate to the **R**. Take this across the field then head **L** downhill, onto the fast singletrack descent (watch the gate!), dropping down to the village of Bradwell.

5 Head downhill into the village, and onto the main road. Turn **R**. Through the traffic lights and **SA** before turning **L** onto Town Lane, just before the small football field. Keep **SA** onto a signed bridleway which weaves its way through the cement works, to eventually emerge onto a tarmac road. Turn **R** and follow the road back into the village of Hope. Turn **L** to the car park.

04 DARK & WHITE

JOHN HORSCROFT ABOVE GRANGEMILL

05 **Grangemill**

Introduction

A good circuit to do when the rest of the Peak is sitting under a veil of mud. With plenty of fast sections, and limited opportunity for mud to form, this circuit is a good winter trip, or indeed a good beginner ride. For a long and fast ride, link it with the Middleton Circuit, fit your semi-slicks (or grab the CX bike) and see how quickly you can do it.

The Ride

Starting off with a blast along the High Peak Trail, the ride cuts off across country, mostly on good tracks, with a field or two, before dropping into Grangemill. Pleasant lanes gain height again, with a section of farm track leading you back to the start to complete the circuit.

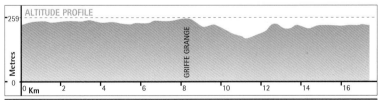

ALTITUDE PROFILE

GRIFFE GRANGE

259

Metres

0

0 Km   2   4   6   8   10   12   14   16

GRANGEMILL   GRADE: ▲

TOTAL DISTANCE: 17KM » **TOTAL ASCENT:** 366M » **TIME:** 1.5-2.5 HRS » **START/FINISH:** CHAPEL PLANTATION (HIGH PEAK TRAIL) » **START GRID REF:** SK 195582 » **SATNAV:** PIKEHALL » **PARKING:** MINNINGLOW FREE CAR PARK ON HIGH PEAK TRAIL, NEAR PIKEHALL » **OS MAP:** EXPLORER OL24 THE PEAK DISTRICT – WHITE PEAK AREA » **PUB:** HOLLY BUSH INN, GRANGEMILL TEL: 01629 650 300 » **CAFÉ:** BRING SANDWICHES.

Directions – Grangemill

➊ Leave the car park and head east on the High Peak Trail. Follow this disused railway track for approximately 8km, looking out for Harborough Rocks on the left – a kind of mini Dolomites. 1km further on, the trail starts to run parallel to a road and after 100m, turn **L** on the signed bridleway to Grangemill Head across the field.

2 Cross over some stiles by gates and the trail soon becomes a track. Go **SA** where the track swings left, down a fine fast bridleway to join a larger track. Follow this turning **L**, then downhill, ignoring a leftwards branch up to a farm. Continue down then back up, through some gates, looking out for a signed bridleway to Grangemill on the **R**. Take this (good singletrack) down through the cow field to the crossroads, pub and hubbub of Grangemill.

3 Take the road **L** towards Longcliffe, but after 150m turn **R** up a narrow lane towards Aldwark. Head uphill and go **SA** through the village, taking the lane to the **L** after approximately 1.5km. Follow this lane for 300m, to where it swings left, at Rockhurst Farm. At this point take the farm track off to the **R** and follow this to the road.

4 Turn **L** and head back along the lane to the car park.

◀☉◯☉ Making a day of it

At its west end, the Grangemill circuit briefly joins the Middleton Circuit (see page 29) on a lane near Gotham (GR SK 198586). In the east, it meets the Cromford loop (see page 63) in Grangemill itself (GR SK 243576). Just thought we'd let you know...

05 GRANGEMILL

MANNERS WOOD PHOTO: TIM RUSSON

06 Bakewell Circuit

17km

Introduction

Tearooms, a country house, a golf course and quaint stone footbridges over well-stocked trout streams are no indication of the fast paced XC riding that this circuit offers. Some of the best woodland singletrack, a dollop of up and a dollop of down – enjoy. It is ideal for both the newcomer to mountain biking wanting to know what all the fuss is really about, or for the seasoned pro, wanting an excellent spin out. A competent rider should get round this non-stop, no foot-downs.

The Ride

We start with a reminder of what we are escaping from, but we soon leave the congestion of town and road for a brisk climb over Cracknowl Hill. Next comes a warm-up along the disused railway track of the Monsal Trail. The rest of the ride is a combination of fast tracks, big aerobic climbs, super-fast grassy descents and of course the fantastic Golf Course Hill descent into Bakewell.

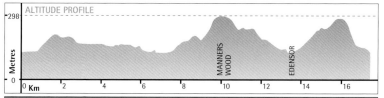

BAKEWELL CIRCUIT GRADE: ▲

TOTAL DISTANCE: 17KM » **TOTAL ASCENT**: 550M » **TIME**: 1.5 HRS+ » **START/FINISH**: BAKEWELL
START GRID REF: SK 220686 » **SATNAV**: BAKEWELL » **PARKING**: LARGE PAY AND DISPLAY
OS MAP: OL24 THE PEAK DISTRICT – WHITE PEAK AREA » **PUB**: PLENTY TO CHOOSE FROM IN BAKEWELL
CAFÉ: THE BAKEWELL PUDDING PARLOUR TEL: 01629 815 107.

Directions – Bakewell Circuit

❿ Exiting the main Bakewell car park, turn **L** and queue with the traffic over the bridge to the roundabout and head **SA** on the A6 signed *Buxton*. After 500m turn **R** just by the speed camera, across a stone footbridge, go **SA** up the track under the old bridge. Climb steadily uphill, taking the **R** fork at the junction. The track levels off then drops down to the Monsal Trail.

2 Turn **R** and follow the trail, rapidly weaving in and out of the prams and pedestrians to its end, some 3km later. Turn off the trail, ignore the tarmac and drop down into the fields towards the river. Follow the bridleway as it weaves along the valley floor, before exiting onto a metalled road. Curve **L** up the road, over the tunnel entrance, watching out for a gate and bridleway off to the **R**, into the field.

3 Up through the field, emerging onto a good fast track. After approximately 1km, pass a track descending to the **R**, in a further 200m you come to a crossroads, ignore the tracks off to the left and right, but go through the gate **SA** and up the dirt singletrack into the woods. Superb, hard but rideable, climbing through the trees, emerges onto a level piece of track, but after a few short metres, breath recovered, branches off again **R** uphill. The track levels off onto fast woodland singletrack; the twisty trail eventually ends at a gate.

4 Through the double gates and downhill, fast and furious, to the woods and another gate, go **R** down the trail (not **SA**) and take the **L** fork where the bridleway splits. Follow the track up across the field and into the woods. **SA** through the woods. Where the track emerges, go **SA** down the parkland (watch those jumps!), aiming for a small clump of trees. Finger posts mark the way. Turn **R** just before the trees and keep going across the Devonshires' front lawn towards the road.

5 Turn **L** down the road, soon branching off to the **L** onto a signed bridleway. Back onto the road, then **L** signed *Edensor Tearooms*. **SA** keeping the church to your left. Up the road, then track, a good honest climb, go **SA** on the road at the top. Just beyond the brow of the hill, immediately after a farm track on the left, and before Ballcross Farm on the right, take the bridleway **SA** steeply down into the trees.

6 Superb descending brings one to the golf course, cross this (danger – imagine the embarrassment of being hit). Rejoin the road, and cruise back downhill to the car park.

◀◼ Making a day of it

Choices, choices, choices. Turn onto the Rowsley loop (see page 131, GR SK 230670) and follow it until the two rejoin in Lees Moor Wood (GR SK 245670) for a mammoth ride. Alternatively, head up the road from Edensor to Pilsley (GR SK 241710) to run round the Calver Circuit (see page 43).

06 BAKEWELL CIRCUIT

© CROWN COPYRIGHT AND/OR DATABASE RIGHT. ALL RIGHTS RESERVED. LICENCE NUMBER 100025218.

07 **Middleton Circuit**

17.5km

Introduction

A companion to the Grangemill ride. When combined, the two make a brilliant ride, taking in quintessential White Peak scenery. This route is a bolder proposition than the Grangemill ride; still a reliable option for the winter, but with more 'real' mountain biking.

The Ride

The route warms up along a quiet lane, then descends into Long Dale, which was once a glacial spillway. Climb out and drop down to Middleton, not quite a remnant from the last Ice Age, but certainly maintaining much olde worlde charm. It is all good fast lanes and well-surfaced disused railways back to the start, but with enough hills to keep the legs interested.

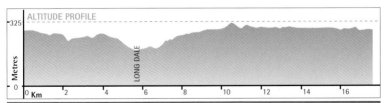

MIDDLETON CIRCUIT   **GRADE:** ▲

TOTAL DISTANCE: 17.5KM » **TOTAL ASCENT**: 344M » **TIME**: 1–2 HRS » **START/FINISH**: CHAPEL PLANTATION (HIGH PEAK TRAIL) » **START GRID REF**: SK 195582 » **SATNAV**: PIKEHALL » **PARKING**: MINNINGLOW FREE CAR PARK ON HIGH PEAK TRAIL, NEAR PIKEHALL » **OS MAP**: EXPLORER OL24 THE PEAK DISTRICT – WHITE PEAK AREA » **PUB**: THE FARMYARD INN, YOULGREAVE TEL: 01629 636 221 » **CAFÉ**: BRING SANDWICHES.

Directions – Middleton Circuit

⤷ From the car park, go back onto the road and turn **L**, heading up what is Mouldridge Lane, soon joining the main A5012. Turn **R** and follow the road for 300m, before taking the bridleway off to the **L**. Follow this as it becomes a great little descent into Long Dale. Keep **L** where the trail splits, heading up the floor of Long Dale. Easy going becomes hard going as the trail starts to climb up and out of the dale. Where the track levels off, head **R** over to the wall.

2 Go through the gate and onto a more distinct track. Follow this, through more gates, looking out for a singletrack branching off **L** as the track swings round to the right. Take this narrow bridleway, emerge onto the road and keep **SA** into the village of Middleton.

3 Turn **L** at the crossroads, climbing steeply uphill, taking the **L** fork, still on tarmac, after approximately 300m. Follow this, Whitfield Lane, soon deteriorating into rough track. Drop downhill to a T-junction, just in front of a large house, head **R**, not left – that only leads to Mount Pleasant Farm. Follow the track to where it meets the road.

4 Turn **R** for 800m up to the crossroads, then turn **L** along the track. Keep **SA** on Green Lane, to where it crosses the High Peak Trail. Turn **L** onto the High Peak Trail. Follow the excellent and fast disused railway line for about 5km back to the car park.

⤙◎◎ **Making a day of it**

The Middleton Circuit briefly joins the Grangemill circuit (see page 21) on a lane near Gotham (GR SK 198586). Join the two for a big old ride. Alternatively, it runs along the High Peak Trail for a short way. Not in any way technical, but a nice way to see the sights and get some miles in, this can be followed in either direction for as long as your legs will carry you.

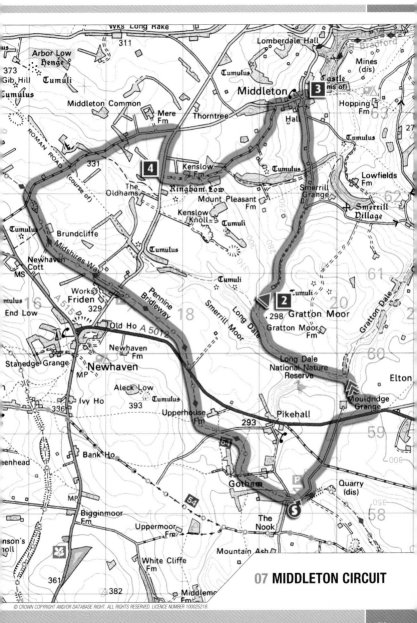

07 MIDDLETON CIRCUIT

Introduction

The riding along the eastern edge of the White Peak, north and south of Linacre reservoirs, couldn't be more different to that found deeper into the National Park's Dark heart. Gone are the brooding moors and rough gritstone trails, replaced instead with hidden singletracks linking farms and villages, and quiet lanes commuting the mountain biker between tree-lined limestone trails.

A sister to the Holymoorside ride found later in the book, and effectively a shorter version of the Linacre Classic, this ride packs in much of what is good about this side of the Peak, but it can be a real love or hate ride depending on the height of the vegetation and the amount of mud (there's a hint there, as to when to ride it).

The Ride

Heading south from the reservoir, through the village of Old Brampton, fast tracks and slow hills lead round to Wigley, from where a superb descent leads to a tough little climb north to Birley. The ride continues north making its way up hill and down dale on a variety of tracks and singletrack trails into the village of Holmesfield. The downhill leg is just that, with most of the ups done on the road, leaving fast trails to test the concentration, down to Barlow, on to Cutthorpe and back to the reservoirs.

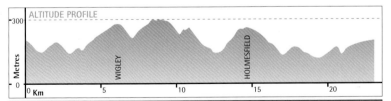

ALTITUDE PROFILE

Metres — 300 — 0

0 Km — 5 — 10 — 15 — 20

WIGLEY

HOLMESFIELD

LINACRE NORTH GRADE: ▲

TOTAL DISTANCE: 23KM » **TOTAL ASCENT**: 693M » **TIME**: 2-3 HRS » **START/FINISH**: LINACRE RESERVOIRS, OFF THE B6050
START GRID REF: SK 334729 » **SATNAV**: S42 7JW » **PARKING**: PAY AND DISPLAY, LINACRE RESERVOIRS
OS MAP: EXPLORER OL24 THE PEAK DISTRICT - WHITE PEAK AREA » **PUB**: THE PEACOCK INN, CUTTHORPE TEL: 01246 232 834
CAFÉ: ICE CREAM VAN AT THE CAR PARK ON NICE DAYS.

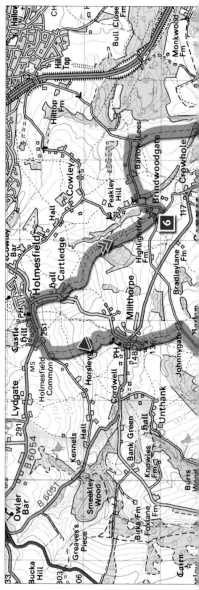

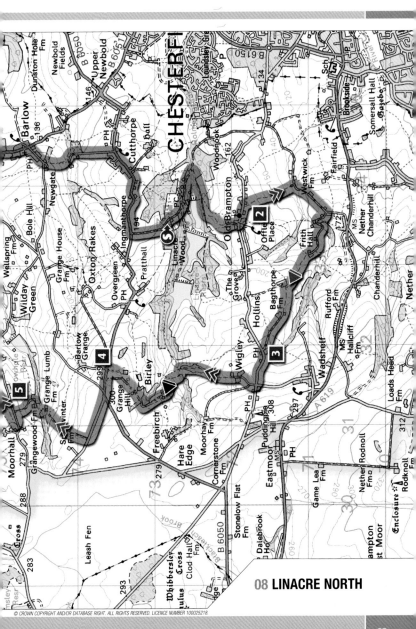

08 LINACRE NORTH

➎ Turn **R** out of the car park (first parking bay on the right as you head down the lane from the main road) and head downhill into the woods, going **SA** as you pass the ranger station on the left. Take the bridleway uphill coming in at an acute angle from the **R** (just after the bridge) and head up through the trees and out into the open, to eventually meet a road. Turn **L** down the road for approx. 200m and then turn **R** onto a bridleway.

2 Descend to the stream and take the track **R** at the T-junction. Follow this uphill, before turning **R** back downhill, where the track turns to tarmac. Follow this, past the farm and onwards and uphill to meet the road.

3 Turn **L** and then take the next **R** signposted to Wigley. Follow the lane around to the right and bear **L** down the bridleway by the stone toadstool. Twisty, rooty, exciting descending leads to the stream. Cross this and climb back out up to Birley Farm as the path turns to a mown strip of grass. Turn **R** off the drive through a gate and across the field (don't stay on the drive!). Through a gate at the far side back onto the lane, and then **R** shortly afterwards through another gate into trees. Follow this **SA** onto a track and up the hill towards the road, staying left at the farm.

4 . Turn **L** onto the road and bear **R** (effectively **SA**) at the junction. After approximately 1km take a track on the **R** down to Grange Lumb Farm. Go past the farm (heeding the *Slow Down* signs) and down **L** into the trees. Cross the stream, head out the other side and emerge on a tarmac farm track and head uphill to the road.

5 Turn **L** on the road and then **R** shortly afterwards on a signed byway – Johnnygate Lane. Meet tarmac and keep **SA**. Look out for a signed byway off to the **L** by some houses; take this to descend over a couple of fords into the village of Millthorpe. Go more or less **SA** over the road onto Millthorpe Lane, and after 150m take the bridleway off to the **L**, by the bus stop. Turn **R** at the top and then **R** at the T-junction onto the main road into Holmesfield. Head through the village, past the pub and church and at the mini roundabout turn **R** down to Cartledge. Bear **L** onto the bridleway in the centre of the hamlet. Great descent, but **take care** as it's a popular trail with other users.

6 Turn **L** at the bottom, keep **L** at the junction and climb for 300m. Turn **R** onto track signed *Unsuitable for Motor Vehicles* and climb to road. Turn **R**. After 800m turn **R** onto signed bridleway – Gateland Lane – as road bends left. Keep **SA** to meet tarmac. Continue **SA** and bear **L** onto main road. Turn **R** after 400m up Wilkin Hill and then **L** after 300m onto a bridleway. Drop and climb to Common Lane and turn **L** (**SA**) into Cutthorpe. Turn **R** on the main road, and then **L** after 1.2km back to the reservoir car park.

SECTION 2

Enduros

Now we're talking. These are big, tough rides (for big, tough riders?) that'll take you a good few hours. They're challenging routes for fit and experienced mountain bikers – you know, 'proper' rides. Rides you might describe as 'a bit of a beast'.

EASTERN MOORS BRIDLEWAY ABOVE CURBAR EDGE

SINGLETRACK DESCENT TO BERESFORD DALE

BELOW BASLOW EDGE PHOTO: TIM RUSSON

09 Calver Circuit

20km

Introduction

Just for a change we've started at the top of a hill, but this is a short enough ride to prevent the last climb at the end from being too painful. The terrain is a real contrast between the fast, loose quarry tracks, some fantastic narrow limestone lanes and paths, and a loop of technical delight around the gritstone of Baslow Edge.

The Ride

Starting off with a wonderful fast chug over crag and moor, the route soon doubles back under Baslow Edge taking in superb technical singletrack before a road descent to Curbar and Calver villages. A grind up to Longstone Edge precedes a great mix of terrain as one traverses between the picturesque villages of Rowland, Hassop, Pilsley and Baslow. The final big long climb back up to Baslow Edge earns a choice of finishes back along the top of Baslow Edge, or back underneath (our choice almost every time!).

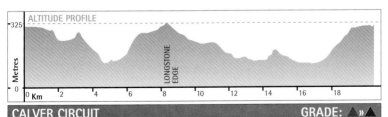

CALVER CIRCUIT **GRADE:** ▲»▲

TOTAL DISTANCE: 20KM » **TOTAL ASCENT**: 620M » **TIME**: 2 HRS+ » **START/FINISH**: CURBAR GAP
START GRID REF: SK 267747 » **SATNAV**: CURBAR » **PARKING**: PAY & DISPLAY, CURBAR GAP
OS MAP: EXPLORER OL24 THE PEAK DISTRICT – WHITE PEAK AREA » **PUB**: THE MOON, STONEY MIDDLETON TEL: 01433 630 203
CAFÉ: WEEKEND SNACK VAN, CURBAR GAP CAR PARK.

Directions – Calver Circuit

↪ Turn **R** out of the car park, ignore the first track on the **L**, but take the second, just beyond the brow of the hill. Through the gate, keep to the **L** on the main track, and race along the moor top. Turn **R** at the end, just after passing the prominent Eagle Stone on the left, passing the first small quarry and fork **R** underneath the next quarry (**easy-to-miss**: it's before the gate and descent proper). Follow this track down, fork **R** at a path junction and then along under Baslow Edge. Variously technical and interesting. Continue more or less **SA** to meet the road.

2 Turn **L** down the road and through the village. Turn **R** at the bottom, then **R** onto the main road. Along the road for a short distance, then turn **L** into Calver Village. Follow the road, past the post office, then climb steeply to the main Bakewell road. Turn **L** onto the road and after 100m turn **R** to a wide gravel track and gate. Climb steeply up and up. Eventually meeting a T-junction near buildings, turn **R**. Take the large track off to the **L** after 500m, keeping the large quarry to your left.

3 Descend the track, eventually joining tarmac and the village of Rowland. Pass through the village, turn **L** at the T-junction and drop down to Hassop, turning **R** at the junction. **Easy-to-miss**: almost immediately turn **L** up the gravel farm track hidden behind a building, past the hens, through the gates, then down the rocky rollercoaster to the ford. Briefly up through the woods then along singletrack to the road.

4 Turn **R** onto the road and take the first **L** up the gravel track which soon levels out to emerge into Pilsley. Ride **SA** down the road and turn **L** at the T-junction to the large roundabout. Take the first exit into Baslow, **R** at the next small roundabout, and then **SA** up into the village.

5 Pass the church and the Spar shop on the left, then go **SA** up Bar Road, and keep those pedals spinning all the way up. Turn **L** at the T-junction halfway up, to Baslow Edge. Either reverse the outward route back along the wide track, or re-ride the singletrack below the edge, turning **R** at the road uphill back to the car park.

⫘ **Making a day of it**
Turn off the ride at Calver (GR SK 239748) and join the Great Longstone route (see page 59) to rejoin the Calver Circuit near Rowland (GR SK 213721).

09 CALVER CIRCUIT

DESCENT TO FROGGATT EDGE

Introduction

A last minute addition this one, thanks to the wonderful work being carried out by the Eastern Moors Partnership (National Trust and RSPB) and Ride Sheffield, opening up access for cyclists and horse riders and generally encouraging all users to enjoy these wonderful moors. A year before publication the Barbrook Valley trail was a no-go for bikes, and the path along Curbar and Froggatt Edges was only upgraded as we checked our final proofs. These two trails have filled the previously bridleway/byway-less void between Blacka and Totley, and the White Peak trails to the south. On a busy weekend day, you'll be sharing the trails so be sure to smile, say 'hi' and enjoy the cracking views along the gritstone edges.

Find out more: www.easternmoors.org.uk

The Ride

This is a fairly zippy ride, without too much in the way of ascent and descent, but it is a great ride, passing over lovely moorland and along the fine gritstone trail above Curbar and Froggatt Edges. From the lay-by near The Grouse pub (mmm, steak pie) head up the road before picking up a bridleway on the right. Climb up to the Owler Bar Road and loop over Totley Moor before heading south to the tranquil Barbrook Valley. Whizz briefly on the road and head over to Baslow where you can drop under the edge on singletrack, or stay on the crag-top path. Pass over Curbar Gap onto the Curbar crag-top path and cruise along, with fun jumps along the way. The drop from Curbar to Froggatt provides the ride's technical interest, before more cruising back to the A625 and the car. Yay for a forward-thinking, modern approach to countryside access!

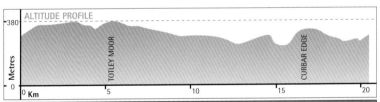

EASTERN MOORS TOUR   **GRADE:** ▲»▲

TOTAL DISTANCE: 20KM » **TOTAL ASCENT**: 380M » **TIME**: 1-2 HRS » **START/FINISH**: LAY-BY BY THE GROUSE, ON A625 » **START GRID REF**: SK 257778 » **SATNAV**: S11 7TZ » **PARKING**: LAY-ON A625, OR NATIONAL TRUST NETHER PADLEY PAY & DISPLAY » **OS MAP**: EXPLORER OL24 THE PEAK DISTRICT – WHITE PEAK AREA » **PUB**: THE GROUSE INN, FROGGATT TEL: 01433 630 423 » **CAFÉ**: WEEKEND SNACK VAN, CURBAR GAP CAR PARK; LONGSHAW CAFE, JUST OFF ROUTE TEL: 01433 637 904.

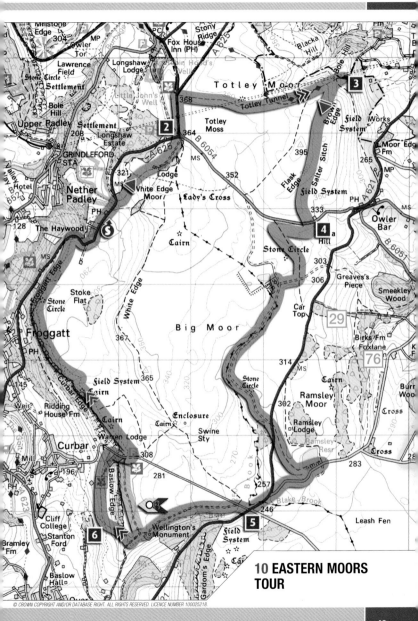

10 EASTERN MOORS TOUR

Directions – Eastern Moors Tour

❻ From the lay-by (or NT car park) ride up the A625 past the Grouse Inn and take the second bridleway on the **R**, just after the bend. Climb steadily on a grassy trail heading for White Edge Lodge. Pass to the **R** of the lodge, onto the drive and take this to meet the road at the junction of the A625 and B6054.

2 **Carefully** negotiate this busy junction so as to head effectively **SA** on the A625 in the direction of Fox House/Sheffield. After 500m, turn **R** signed *Sheffield*, and then turn immediately **R** through a gate onto a bridleway. Follow this for just over 2km, ignoring junctions, level at first and eventually descending fast and rocky to meet a gate at a wall.

3 **Turn around** and ride back up the way you came for approx. 100m (you *could* have stopped on the way down, but why would you?) and take a grassy path forking slightly **L** uphill just after passing a gate on the right. Path climbs and then levels after approx. 800m. Continue **SA**, joining a doubletrack and continue **SA** to meet the B6054 road by a building.

4 Go **SA** over the road, and through a gap in the wall at the left-hand end of the lay-by. Turn **R** through the gate and ride alongside the wall, on a mix of grassy singletrack and surfaced trail. After about 400m, just before a wide gate in the wall on the right, turn **L** onto a wide grassy track and follow the Eastern Moors bridleway markers. Fork **R** after 500m to meet a tarmac lane and turn **R** onto this towards the house. Turn **L** onto the Barbrook Valley bridleway and follow this for over 2km to meet the A621. **Carefully** cross the A621, go through the gate opposite and follow the trail around Ramsley Moor. Watch out for a marker pointing **R** and follow this down to the road. Turn **R** down the road and then **L** at the A621 for a couple of hundred metres. (There are plans to open a bridleway which cuts the corner here, thereby missing the A621 entirely.)

5 Turn **R** at the crossroads and then **L** onto a signed byway at the top of the small hill. Follow this for 1.5km towards Baslow Edge. *Keep **SA** and descend past a bench. Turn **R** not long after the bench, through a small quarry and drop fast below Baslow Edge.

> *(wet weather option)
> Turn **R** shortly after Wellington's Monument along the broad track above
> Baslow Edge to join the Curbar Gap road. Continue **SA**, rejoining the directions
> midway through point 6.

6 **Easy-to-miss:** after 500m, turn **R** at a signed junction onto the bridleway below Baslow Edge. Follow this, technical and/or boggy in places, depending on time of year, through a couple of gates, to join the Curbar Gap road. Turn **R** up this and then sharp **L** at a wide track towards the top. Climb to a gate, through this and onto the Curbar–Froggatt bridleway. After about 1.2km, keep **R** as all hells breaks loose as it descends towards Froggatt – this is the official bridleway, straight ahead is much more technical. Keep **SA** above Froggatt, eventually joining the A625. **Carefully turn R** onto the road and climb back to the lay-by/NT car park.

⛓ Making a day of it

This ride is ideal for linking into the Blacka and Totley Moor riding found just north in the Dark Peak (see our companion *Peak District Mountain Biking* guidebook) or into a variety of White Peak Rides: to the east, the various Linacre riding (pages 9, 33, 75 and 119); and to the south and west the Calver, Great Longstone and Bakewell rides (pages 25, 43, 59 and 81).

Introduction

Upon researching this ride, checking the maps, and knowing the terrain, I thought we were basically in for another one of those 'tracks 'n' roads' type rides: all very energetic, great views, but lacking in any real challenging mountain bike riding. How wrong I was. This ride is surprisingly good. It packs in a huge amount of quality singletrack, great ups and superb downs. The terrain is some of the best the Peak can offer, and despite a chunk of it being on the Pennine Bridleway, it is essentially unspoilt, hardcore riding.

The Ride

The River Wye cuts a deep trench through the limestone of the Peak, with remarkable bridleways traversing and transecting it at several points – as does a disused railway line, which provides a pleasant warm up round towards Monsal Head. The mountain biking proper kicks in with a state-of-the-art hill climb above Monsal Dale that will test the best. The reward is some fantastic views and a pleasant traverse around to the Pennine Bridleway. The drop down into and climb out of Cheedale is mega, while some fantastic double and singletrack takes you back round to Miller's Dale.

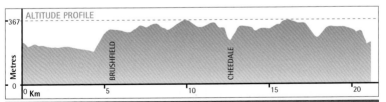

CHEEDALE & THE WYE VALLEY   GRADE: ▲ » ▲

TOTAL DISTANCE: 21.5KM » **TOTAL ASCENT:** 810M » **TIME:** 2.5 HRS+ » **START/FINISH:** MILLER'S DALE STATION
START GRID REF: SK 138732 » **SATNAV:** SK17 8SN » **PARKING:** MILLER'S DALE PAY AND DISPLAY
OS MAP: EXPLORER OL24 THE PEAK DISTRICT – WHITE PEAK AREA » **PUB:** THE RED LION, LITTON TEL: 01298 871 458;
THREE STAGS HEADS, WARDLOW MIRES TEL: 01298 872 268 » **CAFÉ:** OCCASIONAL TEA/ICE CREAM WAGON AT THE START.

CLIMBING OUT OF CHEEDALE PHOTO: TIM RUSSON

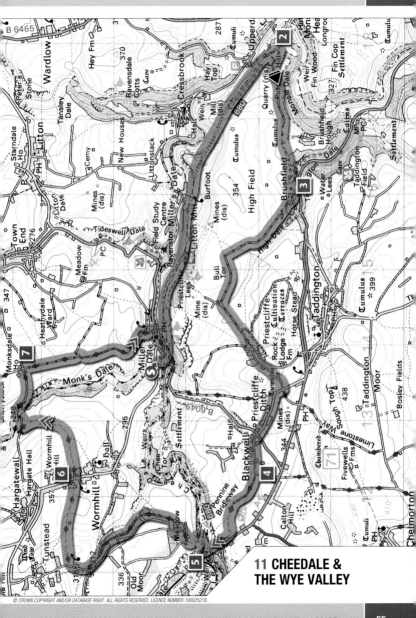

11 CHEEDALE & THE WYE VALLEY

Directions – Cheedale & the Wye Valley

➊ From the car park turn **L** (east) onto the Monsal Trail for approx. 4.5km towards Monsal Head, passing through two tunnels along the way. After the second tunnel, watch out for a good track heading uphill on the **R** signed *Brushfield*, near the old station – take this. If you go under a footbridge you've gone too far.

2 Climb up to the junction, turn **R** uphill onto polished raw limestone. This is one of the classic hill climbs of the Peak. Good luck. The lane eventually flattens out, with fantastic views once you've wiped the blood and sweat from your eyes. Keep **SA** to descend into the hamlet of Brushfield.

3 Keep **SA** up the lane, signed *Priestcliffe*. Keep **SA** on this lane, turning sharp **L**, then downhill, sweeping **L** at the junction with the old-looking New Barn on the right. **SA** to the small village of Priestcliffe. Take the **R** fork in the road, and turn **R** at the next crossroads. Keep **SA** on tarmac, **SA** at the next crossroads, and through the small village of Blackwell.

4 The tarmac starts to deteriorate, ride **SA** onto the Pennine Bridleway where the road swings left. Follow the *Pennine Bridleway* signs, through the distinctive horse-friendly gates and keep **L** at the first junction of tracks (i.e. ignore the track heading off straight downhill). As the track swings back towards the road, keep **L** and follow those gates and the Pennine Bridleway downhill – excellent – over the disused railway, and **SA** down towards the river. Cross this.

5 Turn **R** and follow the excellent grassy track steadily uphill (and up and up) emerging into Mosley Farm. **SA** through the farm, taking the road back out. **SA** up the lane to join the road, then just after a row of cottages and a telephone box on the right, turn **R** onto a track, towards Wormhill. Keep **SA** on this track, which briefly disappears, and **SA** up the hill; keep the wall on your right. Drop through the farmyard; turn **R** onto the road.

6 Almost immediately turn **L** onto the signed public bridleway. Brilliant riding, watch out for the sharp turn **L**, down onto walled singletrack, emerging into the valley bottom of Monk's Dale. Bear **L** to the gap in the wall and the road. Turn **R** uphill on tarmac, turning **R** down a track at the crossroads after the farmhouse, just under 1km from Monk's Dale.

7 Rutty singletrack and doubletrack fun descends with speed and abandon down to the farm – keep up the pace to outrun the dog. Keep **SA** downhill onto a loose and rocky bit of lane. Turn **R** onto the small road, and **SA** onto the main road. **SA** under the viaduct, past the craft shop, then **R** back uphill turning **L** into the car park. Good wasn't it?

◄◉◉ Making a day of it
The bottom of the valley at Monsal Head (GR SK 178718) is the start of the course used in the annual Monsal Head Hill Climb. Detour down to the road and hammer up it as fast as is physically possible and try not to vomit at the top. Anything under two minutes is a good effort, a one-thirty would probably put you a nice way up the rankings.

PHOTO: TIM RUSSON

SINGLETRACK ABOVE COOMBS DALE

12 Great Longstone

18km

Introduction

This ride gives a great flavour of the White Peak, and can even be attempted in the wet winter months as most of the trails are stone based. Great views, some lovely trails and rocky descents all combine to leave the rider wanting more.

Unfortunately we've had to relegate the formerly excellent descent of Wigley Lane to an optional route as it underwent 'maintenance' work by Derbyshire County Council in 2013 and lost all of its White Peak character, with the native limestone inexplicably replaced with tarmac road planings...

The Ride

Limited parking is available in the village of Great Longstone, with alternative parking readily available at Monsal Head, a short ride from the start. The ride begins with a tough little climb onto Longstone Edge before a fine singletrack descends to Black Harry Gate. A short and sharp climb takes you up to Middleton Moor and a warp-speed descent through the quarries to the Stoney road. Climb up into Eyam ... and keep climbing, before the fine reward of the two-part descent back to Stoney: open singletrack through fields at first, before a steep rocky drop into the trees. A long, gentle climb up Coombs Dale drops you back at Black Harry Gate and a singletrack traverse back up to Longstone Edge and the final fast descent to Rowland. Quiet lanes lead the way home.

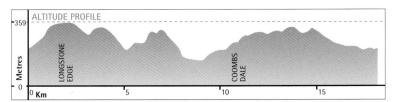

ALTITUDE PROFILE

-359

Metres

LONGSTONE EDGE

COOMBS DALE

0

0 Km   5   10   15

GREAT LONGSTONE   **GRADE:** ▲ » ▲

TOTAL DISTANCE: 18KM » **TOTAL ASCENT**: 650M » **TIME**: 1.5–2.5 HRS » **START/FINISH**: GREAT LONGSTONE
START GRID REF: SK 200717 » **SATNAV**: DE45 1TA » **PARKING**: ON STREET » **OS MAP**: EXPLORER OL24 THE PEAK DISTRICT – WHITE PEAK AREA » **PUB**: THE WHITE LION, GREAT LONGSTONE TEL: 01629 640 252
CAFÉ: PEAK PANTRY, EYAM TEL: 01433 631 293.

Directions – Great Longstone

⟳ Head west out of the village, and turn **R** (effectively **SA**) onto Moor Road on a left-hand bend. Climb above the village onto Longstone Edge.

2 Towards the top, as the track swings left and meets another wide track, turn **R** and then almost immediately **L** though a gate onto a signed Public Bridleway. Ride along the field edge, pass through another gate and descend singletrack to another gate. Continue **SA** through this, along another field edge and through further gates to emerge on a wide track.

3 Ride **SA** up the steep, narrow climb opposite. Continue **SA** over the brow, **SA** across the lane and onto a descent past yet more quarries. Towards the bottom, heed the *Footpath/Bridleway* signs though the quarry and emerge, brakes permitting, slowly on to the busy A623. Go **SA** across the main road and up the minor road to Eyam. Climb up through the village, keeping to the main road.

4 As the houses end, bear **L** up Riley Lane. Keep **R** at the first fork and continue around, past Riley Graves, to the woods. Bear **R** into the woods and descend through fields to the road. Go almost **SA** across the road onto a fast and rocky descent into Stoney Middleton. Follow your nose out to the main road (A623) and turn **L** onto it.

5 After 600m turn **R** up the track immediately after the playing fields. Follow this track up Coombs Dale for about 3.5km, back to Black Harry Gate. Pass through a gate by the small ponds and turn **L** on a wide track and immediately **L** again onto a singletrack bridleway. Follow this back above Coombs Dale for just over 1km.

6 After the gate turn **L*** onto the broad track. As the woodland ends on the right, turn **R** onto a track and then **R** again. Descend to Rowland. Follow the lane through the village and turn **R** at the T-junction. Follow the road back to Great Longstone.

⮞OR *Alternatively, turn **R** after the gate up a climb with a large open quarry to your right. In a dip, turn **L** onto the signed Public Byway – Wigley Lane. At the bottom turn **R** to rejoin the main route into Rowland.

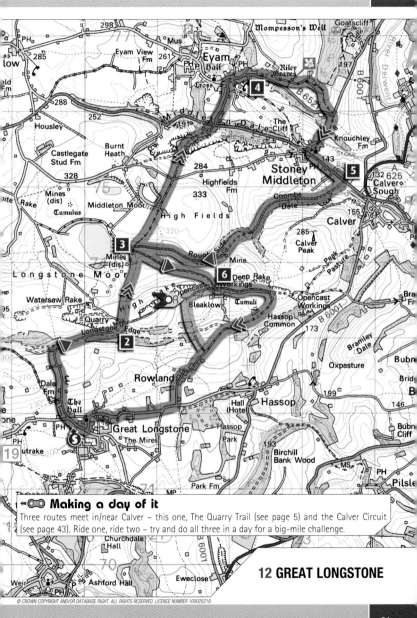

Making a day of it

Three routes meet in/near Calver – this one, The Quarry Trail (see page 5) and the Calver Circuit (see page 43). Ride one, ride two – try and do all three in a day for a big-mile challenge.

12 GREAT LONGSTONE

SINGLETRACK DOWN INTO BONSALL

13 Cromford Circuit

Introduction

What makes a bad ride? Grassy fields, busy roads, overgrown trails, convoluted routes. It is often a fine line between good and bad, not withstanding the day-to-day variables of weather, rider and the like. Some rides can have a heap of the above features, yet still be good, while some can have only a few bad points, but be poor. Of course this is dependent on whether you've got up off the sofa in the first place. I tend to choose a ride either because a) it's my local favourite circuit, b) it's a classic round, c) it's got great technical bits to fit my mood, or d) – and here's the point I'm getting to – it traverses a part of the country I've never seen – it's a tour. This Cromford circuit is a great tour traversing a part of the world few mountain bikers get to. It is a good lap of the area and has some great historic interest.

The Ride

Set off from Black Rocks car park, and warm up (and up and up) westbound along the High Peak Trail. Turn north to Grangemill along fast, satisfying tracks and paths. Roads, tracks and challenging singletrack bring you to a great descent into the village of Bonsall, where a choice of routes lead into Cromford. An excellent fast climb out, followed by a dull grassy field section leads to more good tracks and a descent back to the start.

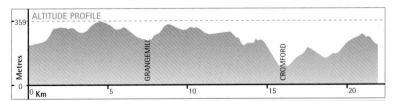

ALTITUDE PROFILE

GRANGEMILL

CROMFORD

Metres

359

0

0 Km   5   10   15   20

CROMFORD CIRCUIT   GRADE: ▲»▲

TOTAL DISTANCE: 21KM » **TOTAL ASCENT**: 675M » **TIME**: 2 HRS+ » **START/FINISH**: BLACK ROCKS, CROMFORD
START GRID REF: SK 290556 » **SATNAV**: DE4 4GT » **PARKING**: BLACK ROCKS CAR PARK » **OS MAP**: EXPLORER OL24
THE PEAK DISTRICT - WHITE PEAK AREA » **PUB**: THE RISING SUN, MIDDLETON TEL: 01629 822 420 » **CAFÉ**: SCARTHIN
BOOKS CAFE, CROMFORD TEL: 01629 823 272; MILL YARD RESTAURANT, ARKWRIGHT'S MILL TEL: 01629 823 256.

MIDDLETON INCLINE

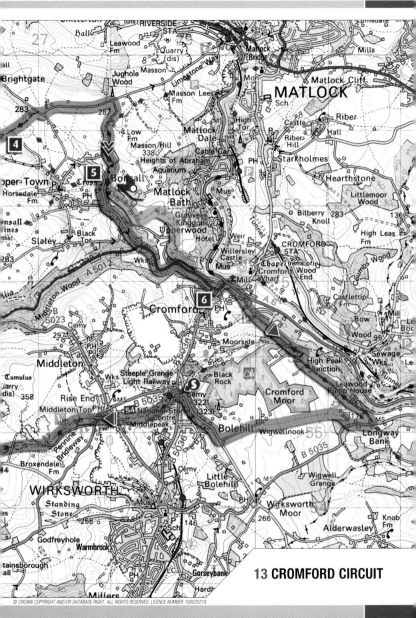

13 CROMFORD CIRCUIT

Directions – Cromford Circuit

❻ From the car park set off on the level cinder High Peak Trail, heading west. Cross the bridge over the road, pass the light railway and over two more roads to a long steady climb up to a viewpoint and a flat fast trail to another climb. The trail levels off, and runs parallel to a road on the left. After a factory and a small building on the left, a signed bridleway heads off across fields to the **R**.

2 Take this (if you reach a gate where the trail diverges from the road you've gone too far). Head across the field, over some stiles by gates and the trail soon becomes a track, which turns left into some large buildings. Go **SA** where the track swings left, down a fine fast bridleway to join a larger track. Follow this turning **L**, then downhill, ignoring a leftwards branch up to a farm. Down then back up, through some gates, looking out for a turn **R** signed *Bridleway to Grangemill*. Take this good singletrack down through the cow field to the crossroads, pub and hubbub of Grangemill.

3 Go **SA** up the road, immediately turning **R** up the lane to Ible. Go **SA** up this road, ignoring the right turn to Ible, and climb steeply past the scruffy farm to a crossroads of lanes and tracks. As the road turns sharp right, turn **sharp L** on the track and descend to the road. Go **SA** across the road onto another broad track towards a large hole in the ground. Either go **SA** and descend into the hole and slog out the other side (along with all the other scrambling types – the fun option), or turn **L** uphill for a short way (the conservative/better option), taking the track on the **R** around the hole, then continue **SA** downhill, passing a gate on the left and the gate on the right leading into the quarry. Then **SA** down the path.

4 Descend Moorland Lane, a narrow walled singletrack, keeping to the main path, swinging **L** then **SA** down to the road. **SA** over the road, and then **SA** up the next road looking out for a track (no sign) on the **R** just after a signed footpath (and also 150m before a signed bridleway leads off left). Follow this track (excellent descent), looking out for a **L** turn just before some rock steps, and the start of the tunnel of trees. Take this **L** turn (actually best to take the second **L**, just after the first, and just after the little rock steps...). Follow the narrow bridleway past a stile on the right.

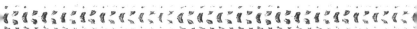

5 The bridleway eventually swings right, turning downhill onto concrete to emerge at the quaint village cross in Bonsall. *Descend on the main road **SA** to a junction with the A5012 and turn **L** to Cromford.

> *From the village cross Church Lane leads off **L**. Follow this, and it soon becomes a bridletrack alongside a quarry. After approx. 1.5km the track splits (the abrupt end of the bridleway), and a **footpath** goes **R** downhill to a zigzag and descent to the main road. Turn **L** to Cromford. **Note:** If you do take this option make sure you observe the right of way of walkers and **push/carry** your bike down this short link-up.

6 Head into the busy world of Cromford. Turn **L** down to the lights and then **R** onto the A6, looking out for a small lane off to the **R** – Intake Lane. Take this, uphill. It eventually becomes a pleasant woodland climb. Under the bridge, the track turns right, then back left to descend past the caravan site to the road. Turn **R**, up the road, looking out for a track down to Meerbrook Farm. Take this, turning off **L** just before the farm, through the gates for a trudge up through the fields, before a good track descends down to a road. Turn **R** and descend into the village, going **SA** where the road turns left, under the bridge and **R** back into the car park.

← Making a day of it

The Cromford Circuit runs briefly along the High Peak Trail. Follow this past the point where the route turns off (GR SK 256546) and you're on the Grangemill circuit (page 21). Keep going and you'll hit the Middleton ride near Gotham (GR SK 198586, page 29). Follow this circuit round, meet the Grangemill ride at roughly the same spot, follow that in reverse to Grangemill itself (GR SK 243576) and finish the original ride.

RICH BARSON IN CUMBERLAND CLOUGH

14 Buxton & the Goyt Valley

Introduction

A superb, scenic excursion into the grit-stone hills of the 'honorary Dark Peak' around Buxton. The loop around the Goyt Valley is a fine example of what might be described as mountain biking lite – testing enough, but rideable all the way for the reasonably fit. An optional loop (recommended) towards the Macc Forest adds more than a little spice, including an exposed high moorland crossing and a superb, loose and rocky descent that leads into the course of Cumberland Brook.

The Ride

Leaving Buxton, the route winds along tarmac before heading off onto the moors. More tarmac, a rocky track around Ladder Hill and a climb from the River Goyt lead to a cruise through the Goyt Valley – all middle ring stuff until you hit the climb up Mill Clough, which is pretty tricky, especially in the mud. Spin through the woods, drop to Errwood Reservoir and take quiet roads through wild-looking scenery. Now either head home on a fast and loose descent to Buxton, or continue past the Cat and Fiddle Inn (lunch stop!) into the wilderness along a rough bridleway into Danebower Hollow. Rock and roll down to Cumberland Clough before scenic back roads climb to a short (but good) descent and a slog back up as a result. Tarmac leads back to a final trip out into the wilds for the rocky finale back down into Buxton.

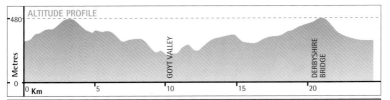

BUXTON & THE GOYT VALLEY **GRADE:** ▲»▲

TOTAL DISTANCE: 25KM (+ 15KM) » **TOTAL ASCENT**: 830M (+ 540M) » **TIME**: 2.5 HRS+ » **START/FINISH**: BUXTON
START GRID REF: SK 058737 » **SATNAV**: SK17 6AQ » **PARKING**: PAY AND DISPLAY, BUXTON STATION
OS MAP: EXPLORER OL24 THE PEAK DISTRICT – WHITE PEAK AREA » **PUB**: CAT AND FIDDLE INN TEL: 01298 78366
CAFÉ: FIVEWAYS CAFE, JUNCTION OF DALE ROAD/LONDON ROAD/HIGH STREET TEL: 01298 72018.

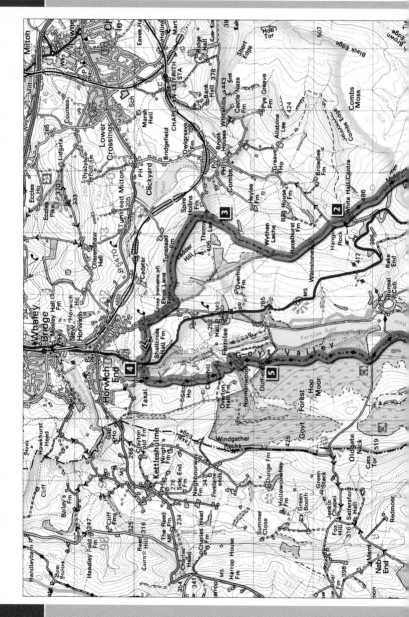

**14 BUXTON &
THE GOYT VALLEY**

Directions – Buxton & the Goyt Valley

☛ Turn **R** out of Buxton railway station car park and head downhill to the first roundabout. **SA** to second roundabout, turn **R** uphill onto Manchester Road/Longhill Road (A5004). Climb steadily up the A5004 for 1.5km to just past Cold Springs Farm, where the road bends sharply to the left – continue **SA** onto a narrow track (Roman road/Midshires Way). Climb up and through gate into short-ish technical section and **SA** out across moorland. Descend to White Hall Centre and junction of tracks

2 Ignore doubletrack on left of entrance to White Hall Centre, follow track as it curves down and to the **R**. **SA** along road, ignoring the road that drops down to right, continue along road over brow of hill. Road drops slightly then curves round to **R** – continue to Wythen Lache Farm on right – look out for a gate, just to the **L** of the farm, leading into a walled track. Through the gate, follow walled track to second gate. **SA** through gate, follow track across field to descend with interest to another gate.

3 **SA** through gate, join tarmac, drop down past Thorny Lee, turn **L** onto rutted, stony road (Long Lane) where it meets road heading right uphill. Follow this track to T-junction with tarmac at Old Road. Turn **R**, roll down Old Road on southern edge of Whaley Bridge. Take second **L** into Shallcross Avenue, follow road up past Shallcross Hall Farm then a good fast descent to meet busy Long Hill (A5004) **with care!**

4 Cross road into large lay-by on opposite side. Drop down steep track leading to ford (footbridge on **R** is the sensible option!). Climb steeply up concrete road on opposite side, through churchyard up to Taxal; turn **L** at top. Follow tarmac road climbing gently upwards to reach T-junction overlooking Mill Clough at Overton Hall Farm. Turn **L** for fast, smooth downhill past **RH** hairpin bend, drop down to gate at Madscar Farm. **SA** through gate and down steeply to cross stream at bottom of Mill Clough. Through gate, climb up track for 100m then **R** through gate just before Knipe Farm. Make challenging climb up rutted track to gate. **SA** through gate, follow walled track past roofless barn where track splits – take lower branch **SA** to Oldfield Farm.

5 Continue through farmyard and bear **R** onto hardpack forest road signposted *Hoo Moor*. **SA** through trees to T-junction with tarmac road, The Street. Turn **L**, roll steeply down road to ride south along western side of Errwood Reservoir. **SA** for gradual climb up to Derbyshire Bridge and visitor centre.

6 *At Derbyshire Bridge Visitor Centre, turn **L** off road onto rough track (signposted *Buxton*). Climb up for a short distance, then make excellent, fast rocky descent (take care with your speed/line) to join tarmac at Burbage. Continue descent to traffic lights, fork **L** to roll into Buxton on the A53. **SA** at two roundabouts to reach Buxton railway station car park.

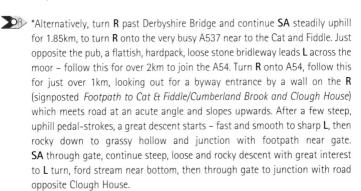 *Alternatively, turn **R** past Derbyshire Bridge and continue **SA** steadily uphill for 1.85km, to turn **R** onto the very busy A537 near to the Cat and Fiddle. Just opposite the pub, a flattish, hardpack, loose stone bridleway leads **L** across the moor – follow this for over 2km to join the A54. Turn **R** onto A54, follow this for just over 1km, looking out for a byway entrance by a wall on the **R** (signposted *Footpath to Cat & Fiddle/Cumberland Brook and Clough House*) which meets road at an acute angle and slopes upwards. After a few steep, uphill pedal-strokes, a great descent starts – fast and smooth to sharp **L**, then rocky down to grassy hollow and junction with footpath near gate. **SA** through gate, continue steep, loose and rocky descent with great interest to **L** turn, ford stream near bottom, then through gate to junction with road opposite Clough House.

Turn **R**, descend to junction, turn **R** onto road. Follow road for approx. 1.5km, past lay-by on left to uphill **L** turn – signposted *Forest Hill/Macc Forest*. At crest of hill, turn **R** on tarmac by entrance to forest, follow road to **L** turn (signposted *Macc Forest*) on tarmac – turn **L** uphill. On entering hamlet of Chapel House, head **R** past the chapel and onto a byway with *No Motor Vehicles* signs. Drop increasingly steeply to the road.

Turn **L** onto the road and keep **L** at the bottom. A brief climb leads to the junction by the pub – turn **R** for a long climb to the A537. At the top, turn **R** onto the A537 for about 800m to the Cat and Fiddle Inn – **take care this is a busy road**. (You might want to note the broad footpath that runs from the tearoom car park almost all the way to the Cat and Fiddle, thus avoiding most of the road – just sayin'.) **SA** past the Cat and Fiddle, turn **L** to descend back on tarmac to Derbyshire Bridge and rejoin at point 6.

15 **Holymoorside**

Introduction

A fantastic technical mountain bike ride with good stretches of challenging singletrack, linked by pleasant stretches of track and lane. Highlights include Harewood Moor, and the singletrack around Linacre reservoirs. Like much of the riding in the area it is best attempted in a dry spring, pre-vegetation, although in moderate conditions only the climb up from Birley Brook is a muddy problem.

The Ride

Starting from Linacre reservoirs the ride warms up easily enough along a pleasant trail, before dropping down to Birley Brook, with interest, to a twisty climb back out that is fantastic – when it's dry. The route then climbs up onto the moors, for some quintessential singletrack action, and a steep, gravelly descent down Hungerhill Lane. More great climbing and fast descending undulates the route north, before a final singletrack descent to the reservoir all too quickly brings the ride to an end.

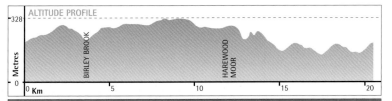

ALTITUDE PROFILE

328

Metres

BIRLEY BROOK

HAREWOOD MOOR

0

0 Km   5   10   15   20

HOLYMOORSIDE **GRADE:** ▲

TOTAL DISTANCE: 21KM » **TOTAL ASCENT**: 570M » **TIME**: 2-3 HRS » **START/FINISH**: LINACRE RESERVOIRS, OFF THE B6050
START GRID REF: SK 334729 » **SATNAV**: S42 7JW » **PARKING**: PAY AND DISPLAY, LINACRE RESERVOIRS
OS MAP: EXPLORER OL24 THE PEAK DISTRICT – WHITE PEAK AREA » **PUB**: THE PEACOCK INN, CUTTHORPE TEL: 01246 232 834
CAFÉ: ICE CREAM VAN AT THE CAR PARK ON NICE DAYS.

HAREWOOD MOOR

➏ From the first parking bay on the right, head **R** downhill for a few metres before taking the bridleway on the **R**, which runs alongside the woods. Go through a gate and **SA** across a field to another gate and a lane which leads to the road. Turn **L** and follow the road for approx. 1km, turning **L** down Birley Road. Follow the lane downhill, going **SA** through the farm onto singletrack. Pass through a gate and turn **L** onto a tarmac lane and then **L** again after 50m through another gate, before big fancy gates, and across a field.

2 Pass through a gate into Birley Farm and go **SA** across the mown strip of grass to pick up the descending singletrack bridleway down to Birley Brook. Cross this, usually boggy for 50m or so, then climb with interest (or cursing guidebook writers if wet) to emerge in Wigley. Continue **SA** to the road.

3 At the road go **SA** through the village of Wadshelf and turn **R** on the main road. After approximately 500m turn **L** for 2.5km to a T-junction (watch out for bison/wildebeest in a field!). At the T-junction go **SA** through a gate onto open moorland and a vague bridleway. Follow this (wooden markers guide the way) to the far corner, before descending to the road.

4 Turn **R** and follow the road for 300m, past a farm on the right, and bear **L** down a track signed *Public Bridleway*. Follow this track down and up and then go left through a double gate and onto superb singletrack across Harewood Moor. **SA** through double gates at the far side and **SA** at a junction of tracks (farmhouse on the left). Carry on to meet Walton Lees Farm. Turn **L** at the farm onto Hungerhill Lane.

5 Descend the track, keeping **SA** at the junction. Descend steeply down Hungerhill Lane, now sadly resurfaced, cross the bridge and climb up to the road. Turn **R** on the road, looking out for a bridleway heading off uphill to the **L** after about 200m. Good technical climbing soon leads to quality singletrack, keep **SA**, eventually dropping down to the road. Turn **R**, downhill, and take the first road on the **L** (Chandler Hill Lane), at the edge of the village.

6 Follow the road uphill and turn **R** at the junction. At the main road, turn **R** and then immediately **L** on the lane just after the garage forecourt. Continue **SA** on a more broken lane and follow this downhill before turning **L** on the bridleway down to the river, just before Broomhall Farm. The track leads down to and across a stream with a pleasant climb up to the road. Turn **L** up the road, past the church, and turn **R** by the red phone box after about 200m. This is a good descent down into Linacre woods. At the track junction by the bridge, turn **L** and climb back up to the car park.

◄⦿◯ Making a day of it
The Holymoorside route could have been called 'Linacre South' as it shares its start/finish car park with the Linacre North ride (see page 33). The two are easily linked.

PHOTO: TIM RUSSON

16 Bakewell Slice

25km

Introduction

You don't get more White Peak than Bakewell, and you don't get much more White Peak than this ride. Pretty villages and grassy fields circled by limestone walls. Woodland singletrack, limestone chatter and wide descents. You pass in front of Chatsworth House and along the former railway lines that once linked the region. And to top it off, the riding's fun too. This is one of the busiest spots in the White Peak, which can mean busy trails, but also means lots of stuff to do when you're not riding.

The Ride

The riding in the Bakewell area is never hugely technical (unless you add the golf course descent) but it is good fun. The riding starts on smooth cyclepaths and runs over rooty singletrack and grassy fields to clattery limestone-strewn descents. The views are good year-round and, when the sun's out and the hedges green (but not too overgrown), it's a lovely place to be. There's a great shortcut/extension which adds a brilliantly tricky descent (watch the rut!) and pubs in virtually every village along the way. So what's the downside? The climbing – it only comes in one form, and that's steep. Still, if you don't mind a bit of effort and want a couple of hours through the centre of the White Peak, this is a good option.

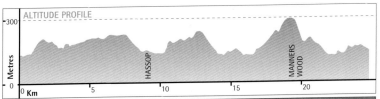

ALTITUDE PROFILE

Metres — 300 / 0

0 Km — 5 — 10 — 15 — 20

HASSOP

MANNERS WOOD

BAKEWELL SLICE   **GRADE:** ▲

TOTAL DISTANCE: 25KM » **TOTAL ASCENT:** 555M » **TIME:** 1.5–3 HRS » **START/FINISH:** BRIDGE IN BAKEWELL
START GRID REF: SK 219686 » **SATNAV:** DE45 1DU » **PARKING:** LOTS IN BAKEWELL
OS MAP: EXPLORER OL24 THE PEAK DISTRICT – WHITE PEAK AREA » **PUB:** IN EVERY VILLAGE BAR EDENSOR!
CAFÉ: IN BAKEWELL, SHOP IN PILSLEY, CAFÉ AT CHATSWORTH AND CALTON LEES.

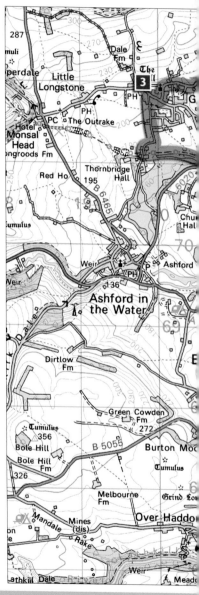

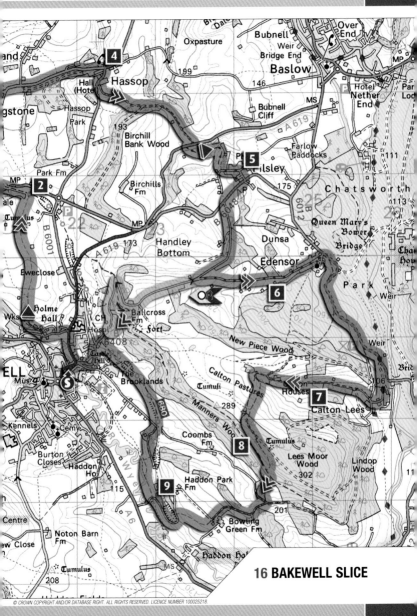

16 BAKEWELL SLICE

Directions – Bakewell Slice

⊙→ Starting from the bridge on the main road in Bakewell, ride away from the town centre, staying on the main road. Pass the 'meadow' on the left and then turn **L** up Holme Lane. Follow this until it 'ends' at a private road sign. Turn **R** up a good track. Pass between buildings and ignore turnings to follow the track uphill through trees and a gate to fields. Cross the field and keep **SA** through the gate ahead. Continue **SA** on narrower tracks, passing through more gates and going over the top of the hill. Follow singletrack downhill to a gate and the Monsal Trail (former rail line, now recreational trail).

2 Turn **L** and ride for 1.5km until, just after passing under a bridge, you reach the old station at Thornbridge Hall. Leave the trail on the **RH** platform and climb the stairs on the **R**, signed to *Great Longstone*. At the road, turn **L** and follow the lane into Great Longstone.

3 In the centre of the village, turn **R** on the main road. Just after the White Lion, turn **L** up Church Lane, towards Rowland and Hassop. Follow this road, ignoring turnings, for 2.5km, to a T-junction in Hassop.

4 Turn **R** towards Bakewell. Ride 100m around two corners and then turn **L** onto a signed byway just after the farm buildings (**easy-to-miss**). Keep **SA** through the farmyard and gates onto singletrack. Rattle down to the stream, splash across and swing left to climb up and out through fields to the road. Turn **R**. Just after the *13 Bends* sign, turn **L** onto a wide track. Go through a gate and climb steeply. Keep **L** at the top of the climb into Pilsley.

5 At the T-junction, turn **R**, and then **R** again at the main road. Climb over the brow of the hill and turn **L** onto a smaller lane (*Unsuitable for Motor Vehicles*). Climb steadily (good views). Just before a steep, straight section, turn **L*** onto a wide track.

▷◁▷ *Extension: The 'golf course' descent is rooty, rutted and technical – great fun. For a shortcut home, or to a couple of extra kilometres, continue on the road over the top of the hill. As you begin to descend and as you reach woodlands, turn **L**/keep **SA** onto a signed bridleway (ignore tyre tracks leading left). Follow singletrack downhill to the golf course. Go **SA** across this, ducking if necessary. At the road, either continue **SA** into Bakewell, or turn **R** and climb steeply to re-join the main route.

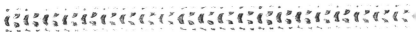

6 Follow the track downhill into the pretty village of Edensor. Keep **SA** through the village to the main road. Turn **R** on the grass and follow a grassy 'shelf' to cut the road corner, re-joining the road higher up. (If it's wet, it may be easier to take the road.) Follow the road through scenic fields in front of Chatsworth House and climb up and over the hill. Descend, cross a cattle grid and turn **R** to Calton Lees. Follow the road past the car park and around to the right. At the junction, keep **SA** through a gate following a wide, signed bridleway into fields.

7 Follow the track along the bottom of grassy fields until a couple of steep zigzags climb through between buildings. Keep to the main track, go through the gate above the buildings and turn **L** along the bottom edge of the field. At the end of the field, turn **L** through a gate. Follow the track until it peters out and bear **L** off onto vague grassy singletrack. Cross the field, aiming for a gate into the woods. Go through the gate and follow wide and obvious singletrack around to the **L**.

8 Wide singletrack runs along the top of the woods, soon dropping to a wider track. Bear **L**, then, just before a gate, bear **R** and drop to leave the woods and join a wide track. Keep **SA**. At a T-junction, keep **R** towards Bakewell. On a sharp right-hand bend by buildings, go **SA**, following bridleway signs through gates to cross the field and re-join the track. Turn **L**.

9 As you round a left-hand bend near the bottom of the valley (just before a bridge), turn **R** through a gate onto a signed bridleway. Follow low wooden bridleway markers along the bottom of the field. As you reach the end of the field, bear **R** to cross the field to a gate and join a good track. Turn **L** along this. At the junction, turn **L**, then quickly **R** to join the Monsal Trail. Follow this until you pass under a bridge and reach buildings. At the far end of the first building reached (a former station), turn **L** through a narrow passage into a car park. Join the road and turn **L**. This leads downhill to the centre of Bakewell.

BERESFORD DALE

17 Manifold Valley

24.5km

Introduction

If you want to tick every corner of the White Peak and you enjoy a good high-speed romp across some stunning Peak District landscape then this is essential riding. If you are new to mountain biking, or indeed have the family along for the day, then you've come to the right place. If you want hardcore trails and demanding terrain, this isn't the route. This ride is more or less split into thirds, good quality singletrack, quiet easy going tracks and lanes, and paved cycleway. On a quiet evening I often pick this route for its solitude and peaceful snapshot of the flora, fauna and environment of the Peak.

The Ride

Starting from beside the village duck pond in Hartington, this ride heads up over a spur of Wolfscote Hill and then back down the dry valley of Biggin Dale, with a short push back out the other side. This is followed by a challenging drop into Beresford Dale and then a climb up around Narrowdale Hill before grand views and speedy descending takes you into the Manifold Valley, among a peloton of family cyclists, up to Hulme End. Quiet lanes and a bit of retracing your steps take you back to Hartington.

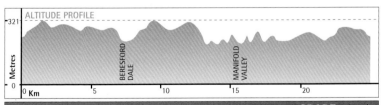

ALTITUDE PROFILE

321

Metres

BERESFORD DALE

MANIFOLD VALLEY

0

0 Km — 5 — 10 — 15 — 20

MANIFOLD VALLEY   **GRADE:** ▲ » ▲

TOTAL DISTANCE: 24.5KM » **TOTAL ASCENT**: 770M » **TIME**: 2 HRS+ » **START/FINISH**: HARTINGTON
START GRID REF: SK 128604 » **SATNAV**: SK17 0AL » **PARKING**: ON STREET IN VILLAGE CENTRE
OS MAP: EXPLORER OL24 THE PEAK DISTRICT – WHITE PEAK AREA » **PUB**: THE DEVONSHIRE ARMS, HARTINGTON
TEL: 01298 84232 » **CAFÉ**: BERESFORD TEA ROOMS, HARTINGTON TEL: 01298 84418.

Directions — Manifold Valley

➊ From the centre of Hartington head east on the B5054, taking the first **R** uphill on High Cross Lane, signed *Youth Hostel*. Go past the hostel and take the lane **R** after approx. 150m. Follow this well surfaced lane **SA** up and then down to join the road. Keep **SA**, taking the first **R** uphill, and then steadily down looking out for a signed bridleway on the **R**; take this.

2 A fun descent leads down into the dale. Turn **R** at the bottom, heading up the dale, then follow the bridleway up the steep hill, onto a better track and then a lane. Keep **SA** for 500m, and then take the byway **L**, down the rocky trail to the road. Turn **R**, and then first **R** down into Beresford Dale.

3 Go **SA** across the bridge. Turn **R** and follow the singletrack to a gate and keep **SA** up the dale. Turn **R** at the junction and follow the track up to the farm, at the base of the conical Narrowdale Hill. At the farm turn **L**, up the track between the buildings then **SA** through gates and steeply uphill. Where the trail levels off, and before the first stone stile, turn **R** up to the hill, then follow the bridleway back **L** and then down the good track, past the camping barn to a T-junction of tracks. Turn **R** to the road.

4 Turn **R** along the lane for 400m, then **L** down the lane, **L** at the T-junction and **SA** into the village of Wetton. Turn **R** at the T-junction in the village, then take the first **L**. Keep **R** at the next junction, descending the steep road towards the Manifold Valley, with good views of Thor's Cave on the opposite side of the dale.

5 Follow the dale upstream to Wettonmill. Turn **R** to the mill, then take the track **L** heading upstream for a couple of gentle kilometres before once again joining the road. Head **R** and then, after about 1km, down **L** across the river and onto the family cycleway upstream to Hulme End. Turn **R** on the road then take the first **R** after 500m. Head **SA** at the crossroads on Beresford Lane down to Beresford Dale. Just before the footbridge over the river, turn **R** along the vague lane across the field. This joins the route out at a gateway – usually with barbed wire instead of a gate.

6 Cross the stile on the right of the gateway, and head acutely back **L** along the narrow trail back down to the bridge across the River Dove. (A good little jump off the end of the bridge.) **SA** uphill, taking the **R** turn on the more amenable wide track up to the road. Turn **L** and follow the lane for 600m taking the track **SA** where the lane swings **R**. Follow the lane to the road, turn **L** downhill, and **L** again back into Hartington.

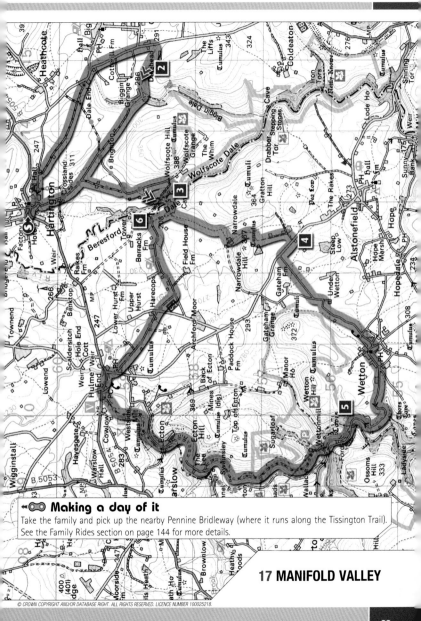

Making a day of it

Take the family and pick up the nearby Pennine Bridleway (where it runs along the Tissington Trail).
See the Family Rides section on page 144 for more details.

17 MANIFOLD VALLEY

18 Gradbach

Introduction

The bridge at Three Shire Heads towards the end of this ride marks the point where Cheshire, Staffordshire and Derbyshire meet. While you'll see a fair few riders here, the likelihood is that they've ventured south from Macclesfield Forest, rather than coming up from Gradbach – the area explored by this ride. Tucked away in the bottom left hand corner of the Peak, it feels more Dark than White – gritstone edges, sandy trails and moorland replacing the usual green fields and woodland. It's obviously similar in this respect to the Macclesfield Forest route on page 107 – and combining the two will give a good big day out.

The Ride

Road, good climb, road, good singletrack, road, good descent ... get the picture? Come ready for tarmac donkey work, the odd tough climb and a whole raft of descents. There's not a lot to say about the road stuff. It gets you from A to B on quiet lanes and the views are nice. The climbs are good: a steep and loose sprint, a long and satisfying drag from Gradbach and a technical challenge near Knotbury. But you're probably most interested in the descents, right? Well, you get the pedal-catchingly technical drop from the Roaches into Black Brook, a rubbly run to Three Shire Heads, and Cumberland Clough – a White Peak highlight that's fast and loose at the top and a blocky tangle further down. It's a great descent that deposits you at your car with a grin, and possibly a pinch flat.

NOTE – Whilst most of this ride is good year-round, there are a few sticky sections that aren't much fun in summer, let alone winter. Wait for dry weather to catch this ride at its best.

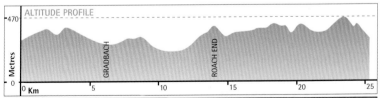

ALTITUDE PROFILE

470

Metres

GRADBACH

ROACH END

0 Km   5   10   15   20   25

GRADBACH   GRADE: ▲

TOTAL DISTANCE: 26KM » **TOTAL ASCENT**: 685M » **TIME**: 2-4 HRS » **START/FINISH**: CLOUGH HOUSE CAR PARK **START GRID REF**: SJ 987699 » **SATNAV**: SK11 0BD » **PARKING**: FREE CAR PARK » **OS MAP**: EXPLORER OL24 THE PEAK DISTRICT - WHITE PEAK AREA » **PUB**: CAT AND FIDDLE, ON THE A537, TEL: 01298 78366 » **CAFÉ**: SANDWICH TIME.

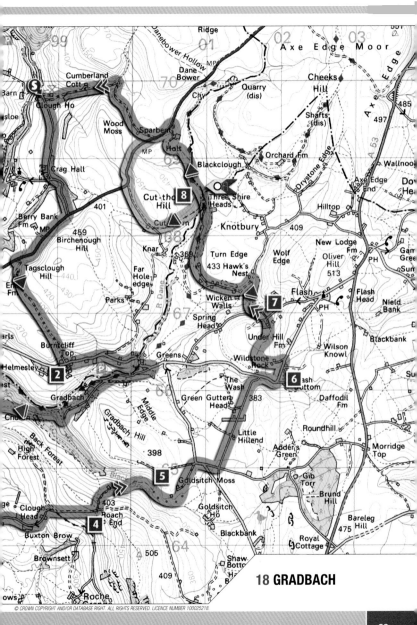

18 GRADBACH

Directions – Gradbach

↱ Turn **R** out of the car park onto the narrow lane. Climb steadily uphill, keeping **L** towards Buxton at the junction. At the main road, turn **R**, towards Congleton. After about 1km, turn **L** through a gate onto a tarmac lane to Heild End Farm. Climb around the hairpin and turn **L** up the rubble climb. Once over the top, keep going straight until you descend to a gate near buildings. Go through the gate down to the road.

2 Turn **L** and speed downhill on lanes. Near the bottom, turn sharp **R**, signed *Gradbach Scout Camp*. Follow the lane to the end – passing turnings to the Scout Camp property and private homes (all signed). Drop downhill to a river. It's probably best **NOT** to try and ford this one, as the rocks are covered with slime and you'll get wet feet. Once across, dry your feet and go **SA** on a wide track signed to *Lud's Church* and *Swythamley*. Climb steadily uphill, past the rocks and up through gates, always keeping on the main track. Begin to descend and then keep **R** through a gate, signed *Swythamley*.

3 Keep **SA** at the junction of driveways and ride to the road. Turn **L**, pass the church and go round the bend before turning **L** up a dead-end road. Climb until the road ends, and then go **SA** on a wide track.

4 At the road, turn **L**, then quickly **L (SA)** again to Roach End Farm. Keep **R** past the farm buildings on grassy singletrack that soon becomes technical.

5 Squeeze across the bridge (how wide are your bars?) and go through the gate into the field. Continue **SA** along the field edge, eventually turning **L** uphill at a sign for *Goldsitch Moss*. **NOTE** – This section can be hideously muddy in winter. At the road, turn **R**, keep **SA** as the road bends right and then turn **L** at the crossroads. Ride to the end of the lane and turn **R**.

6 Climb around the corner and uphill until you are able to turn **sharp L** onto a wide track signed as a bridleway. Follow this **SA** through the farm. Go through gates and into fields. Immediately after a second gate, (with the track petering out about 100m ahead), turn **R** up through the grassy field, alongside the stone wall. Go through a narrow gate and drop to another gate. Pass in front of the house and keep **R** as you ride out to the road.

7 Turn **R** and then quickly **L** down a tarmac drive. Keep **SA** past the house (carefully) and then fork **L** onto a signed bridleway. Good singletrack leads down to a gate and a stream. Cross this and keep **SA** up a loose climb, signed to *Drystone Edge*. Keep climbing **SA** to the road and turn **L**. Pass the motorbike trials area and follow the lane around to the **R**. Fork **R** immediately after the houses and keep **L** at the next fork. A sandy, rocky track leads to the bridge at Three Shire Heads. Cross this.

8 Once over the bridge, turn **R***. Go through the gate and climb a wet and muddy bridleway up the edge of the field. Go through the second gate and then, keeping **R**, go through gates to the farm lane. Turn **L**, uphill. Turn **L** on the main road. After 200m, turn **R** onto a signed byway (optional route rejoins here). Go through the gate and follow the wide track downhill to a gate. Go through this and, always keeping **SA**, drop rockily to another gate and a river. Turn **L** across the river and follow the wide track to the road and the car park.

*This climb gets very muddy. It's only short, but you can bypass it by turning **L** after the bridge, tackling a technical climb and then turning **R** at the lane. At the main road, turn **R** and ride for 700m to re-join the main route above.

19 **South Buxton Circuit**

Introduction

Another corner of the Peak that rarely sees the mountain bike masses, yet is riddled with great trails all the same. Take some time to explore this area and you will be rewarded with good days out around seldom visited little hamlets and quiet byways. Tell someone where you are going and don't speak to the locals!

As part of our main ride we've included a couple of extreme descents – by far the toughest in the area. We've also suggested a shorter, easier optional route which misses out the carnage yet still allows you to explore the area.

You can also get the full lowdown on the Tenterhill/Hollinsclough descents on page 140.

The Ride

Starting with a great view and a blast across the broad valley bottom of the River Dove, the ride then climbs up to the great ridge of limestone south of Buxton, which it traverses west before heading south, past the source of the River Dove. It then drops back down, via a series of extreme rocky steps, to cross the river at Tenterhill, before a push back out, a fine swoopy descent and another crossing at Hollinsclough. Yet more extremely technical downhill terrain (preceded by fierce climbing) leads to a pleasant run back to Longnor.

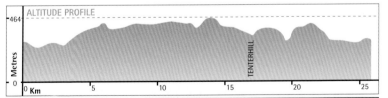

SOUTH BUXTON CIRCUIT GRADE: ▲ » ▲

TOTAL DISTANCE: 15KM/26KM » **TOTAL ASCENT**: 450M/820M » **TIME**: 2–4 HRS » **START/FINISH**: LONGNOR
START GRID REF: SK 088649 » **SATNAV**: SK17 0NT » **PARKING**: LONGNOR CAR PARK
OS MAP: LANDRANGER 119 BUXTON & MATLOCK » **PUB**: THE QUIET WOMAN, EARL STERNDALE TEL: 01298 83 211
CAFÉ: FIVEWAYS CAFÉ, JUNCTION OF DALE RD/LONDON RD/HIGH ST (BUXTON) TEL: 01298 72018.

19 SOUTH BUXTON CIRCUIT

Directions – South Buxton Circuit

↪ From the cobbled parking in Longnor head east out of the village towards Crowdecote and on the edge of town take the **L** turn up the tarmac lane signposted to The Ridge. Follow the track steeply down, pass to the left of a building and then bear **R** across fields and the valley bottom, cross over the bridge and turn **L** upon meeting the farm track at the bend. Go **SA** through the farm and several gates before emerging on the road at Glutton Bridge. Turn **R** and climb steeply up Glutton Dale for approximately 3km, to the brow of the hill and a signed bridleway on the **L**. Take this.

2 Climb steadily on a well-defined grassy track. Pass through a gate, bear **L** across the field, and pick up the track heading **R** through another gate, and another, down to a gate and the road. **Don't go onto the road**, instead take the gate to the **R** and follow the bridleway running parallel to the road. Keep on the raised singletrack line by the fence. Join the road at the next gate by a wide track. Turn **R** on the road and head uphill. Ride round the bend, pass the race track*, up round another hill, and look out for a signed bridleway up a track to the **L** (don't take the left-hand one, downhill).

> *(Shortens the route to 15km/450m, and changes overall grade to blue.) At the race track turn **L** onto a lane and ride for around 600m before turning **R** on another lane, eventually heading downhill towards Booth Farm. Just before the farm fork **L** onto the track (bridleway), keep **L** around the back of the next farm and drop downhill on a fun, swoopy grassy descent. Just before a *Private Property* sign, fork **R** downhill on a narrow singletrack. Carry across the small bridge and ride out up the other side to the road. Turn **L** on the road into Hollinsclough and continue **SA**. At the T-junction turn **L** uphill, and then **R** back into Longnor.

3 Descend the track to Fairthorn Farm, turn **R** in front of the house, up the mown strip of grass, picking up a more defined bridleway which climbs up the valley, with a few tricky bits, before turning **L** to cross the stream and climb up to the road. Turn **L** onto the road and take the **L** fork as the road splits. Descend the lane and turn **R** just after a house with a red phone box outside it (if you cross a cattlegrid you've gone too far). Descend this track to the road.

4 Turn **L** and climb steeply up tarmac to a T-junction. Turn **L** downhill passing two lanes off to the left. After about 2km look out for a signed bridleway to the **L**. Descend this increasingly exciting rutted singletrack to the farm and exit onto the road. Turn **R** downhill, then take the **LH** of the two lanes, bearing **R** in the dip onto singletrack. Take a deep breath, remove that part of your brain which controls logic, tighten the helmet, and award yourself a medal if you reach the stream in one piece. Tenterhill is one of the hardest rocky descents in the Peak, extreme for the last 200m down to the stream. Enjoy. Cross the stream and push your bike back up the other side (heroes *might* be able to ride out...). Ride along the more amenable track to Booth Farm.

5 Keep **R** through the farm and turn **sharp R** immediately after it onto the bridleway. Keep **L** around the back of the next farm and drop downhill on a fun, swoopy grassy descent. Just before a *Private Property* sign, fork **R** downhill on a narrow singletrack. Carry across the small bridge and ride out up the other side to the road.

6 Turn **R** uphill, taking a **L** turn up a very steep track to join a road. Cross this **SA** and follow the good track, soon reaching another road. Turn **L** and climb up to a T-junction. Turn **L** and look out for a good track off to the **L** after 150m. Turn **R** then immediately **L** over the road and pick up the signed byway on the bend down into Hollinsclough. Whatever is left of your bike and skeleton after Tenterhill will not escape trauma on this bad boy of a lane that thinks it's a rockface. Exit onto the road in Hollinsclough.

7 Turn **R** and follow the pleasant road **SA**, to a T-junction. Turn **L** up the steep hill and then **R** back into Longnor.

←🔗 **Making a day of it**

When you reach Tenterhill (GR SK 051673), stop, lower your saddle and turn to page 140 for a play on the various descents in the area. All good fun, especially if you try and ride back up them again...

SECTION 3

Epics

Getting longer now – these loops will take a bit more time and effort. Not rides to be scared of, but definitely rides to be respected. Rather large hills and plenty of technical ground to cover mean that firstly, you're going to be out for a good few hours, and secondly, you're going to have a really good time.

CUT-THORN HILL ON THE MACC FOREST CLASSIC

HAREWOOD MOOR SINGLETRACK

Introduction

A great ride on the far western edge of the Peak District – so far west that it's not even in Derbyshire, sitting as it does just over the border in Cheshire. You'll encounter a third county en route too, as you touch Staffordshire briefly at the lovely Three Shire Heads. But this is a proper mountain biking route: it might sit in the White Peak and on the Ordnance Survey's White Peak map, but it feels very much like its Dark Peak cousins around Edale and the Hope Valley. Big climbs followed by long, rocky, gritstone descents – and what great descents. Charity Lane, misleadingly shown as a lane on the map is a fast rocky plummet, with plenty of rocks to get air off, Danebower Hollow is fast and jumpy, and Cumberland Clough goes from loose and rocky to drops and all sorts in between. The finish is a bit more tame, a high speed grinfest down through Macc Forest.

The Ride

Starting from beside Trentabank Reservoir in Macclesfield Forest, lane work leads to a fire road climb through the northern half of the forest to Charity Lane. A short-ish rocky climb to the summit leads to high speed, rocky fun to the road and a long, but never too steep, climb up to the A537. The stretch across Danebower Hollow feels a little like the Pennine Bridleway in West Yorkshire, before the road is rejoined and you drop to and along the River Dane to Three Shire Heads – a nice spot for lunch. A tough but do-able climb back out to the road leads to Cumberland Clough. It starts off tame enough, but the speed increases as the angle dips. A pootle along the road and a short climb lead to a traverse on fire road around the southern edge of Macc Forest before the final high speed descent to the car.

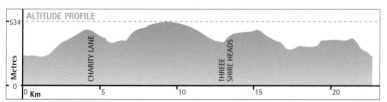

ALTITUDE PROFILE

534

CHARITY LANE

THREEE SHIRE HEADS

Metres

0

0 Km   5   10   15   20

MACCLESFIELD FOREST CLASSIC   GRADE: ▲

TOTAL DISTANCE: 23KM » **TOTAL ASCENT**: 940M » **TIME**: 3 HRS+ » **START/FINISH**: TRENTABANK RESERVOIR, MACCLESFIELD FOREST » **START GRID REF**: SJ 962711 » **SATNAV**: SK11 ONE (NEAREST) » **PARKING**: LAY-BYS OR P&D CAR PARK BY TRENTABANK RESERVOIR » **OS MAP**: EXPLORER OL24 THE PEAK DISTRICT – WHITE PEAK AREA
PUB: LEATHER'S SMITHY, LANGLEY TEL: 01260 252 313; CAT AND FIDDLE INN, A537 BUXTON ROAD TEL: 01298 78366
CAFÉ: NICE NOSH REFRESHMENTS VAN, TRENTABANK CAR PARK (SAT & SUN ONLY).

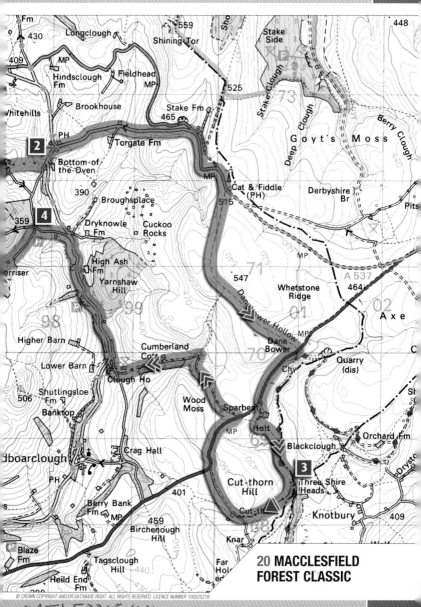

20 MACCLESFIELD FOREST CLASSIC

CAT & FIDDLE INN
SK11 0AR

Directions – Macclesfield Forest Classic

↱ From the road beside Trentabank Reservoir, head down the hill and along the road that separates the two reservoirs. Turn **R** in front of the Leather's Smithy pub, up the lane. After about 600m, as the road bears right, keep **SA** onto a fire road signed *Forest Bridleway*. Climb through the forest for about 1km, avoiding turn offs. When the fire road meets a stone building, bear **R** steeply uphill and curve around left to a gate and tarmac lane. Turn **R** up this. At the top, turn **R** onto a rocky bridleway at the edge of the woods. This is Charity Lane. Climb to the summit and plummet down the other side to meet the road. At the road turn **L**, pass the chapel and onto a byway with *No Motor Vehicles* signs. Drop increasingly steeply to the road.

2 Turn **L** onto the road and keep **L** at the bottom. A brief climb leads to the junction by the pub – turn **R** for a long climb to the A537. At the top, turn **R** onto the A537 for about 800m to the Cat and Fiddle Inn – **take care this is a busy road.** (You might want to note the broad footpath that runs from the tearoom car park almost all the way to the Cat and Fiddle, thus avoiding most of the road – just sayin'.) Opposite the pub, take the signed bridleway for over 2km to meet the A54. Turn **R**, and head downhill for approximately 500m looking out for a tarmac farm track, signed *Bridleway*, off to the left. Turn **L** here and descend towards the farm. Turn **R** up the fenced track, just on the apex of the bend, before the farm. Go through the gate and **SA** down the track, then head **L** and pick up a stream, and more defined tracks, turning **R** at the wall, don't go through the gate. The track descends to the stream. Descend with fun to the bridge at Three Shire Heads.

3 Don't cross the bridge, instead keep **SA** onto a rising, rocky track, which eventually becomes a rather tough climb. At a gate, bear **R** onto a tarmac lane and climb back to the A54. Turn **R**. After 600m, turn sharply **L** by a wall, though a gate onto a byway signed *Public Footpath to Cat & Fiddle Inn*. Follow this, increasingly fast, rough and steep, into Cumberland Clough. Pass through a gate and keep descending before passing through a gate, fording the brook and reaching the road. Turn **R** along the road for about 1.5km, and turn **L** steeply uphill signposted *Forest Chapel/Macc Forest*.

4 At the crest of the hill, go **L** through the gate onto a broad fire road signed *Forest Bridleway*. Climb, then descend and stay on the main track, avoiding turn offs through gates. Climb again and, at a split in the track, turn **L** very steeply up zigzags signed for bikes. Recover your breath and admire the view from the benches at the Nessit Hill viewpoint before returning to the track and a brief, gravel singletrack, again signed for bikes. Keep following the bikes signs and *Forest Bridleway* signs to descend eventually to the road and return along the reservoirs road back to the car.

◄◯◯ Making a day of it

This ride joins up nicely with the Gradbach ride (page 91), taking in the best of both. Alternatively, take the track over Axe Edge Moor (take a map for directions) and make your way over to the South Buxton ride (see page 97) just over the A53 (GR SK 039695). Ride this in reverse to the Traveller's Rest pub (GR SK 032678) and nip down the road through the village of Flash to rejoin the original ride (GR SK 018669).

CUMBERLAND CLOUGH

TIGHT SINGLETRACK NEAR YOULGREAVE

21 Five Dales Circuit

Introduction

This long, hard and varied route is best done in the summer, when the superb woodland singletrack can be enjoyed in all its swoopy finery. The views from Beeley Moor are superb, while the last hairpins on the climb of Rowsley Bar, scene of the National Hill Climb Championship (just over five minutes floor to summit – if you fancy a go) are a great aerobic burn out. However, this is just the beginning, the route keeps heading into and back out of dale after dale, sometimes on super-fast descents, sometimes on singletrack climbs, hard tarmac slogs or just good old honest farm tracks. A brilliant ride, one of the best in this book, taking in all that the heart of the White Peak has to offer.

The Ride

From Darley Bridge, climb out on the long hill east towards Beeley Moor, before a good descent and a big dollop of fine singletrack traverses around to climb back up towards Beeley Moor once again. The route then drops down to cross the River Derwent and climbs to Calton Pastures, before ascending on brilliant woodland trails and crossing the River Wye at Haddon Hall. Steady farm track work leads to yet another great woodland singletrack descent to cross Lathkill Dale, en route to the River Bradford, and so onwards to Birchover, crossing Ivy Bar Brook on the way. A super-fast descent of Oldfield Lane brings the weary rider back to the start.

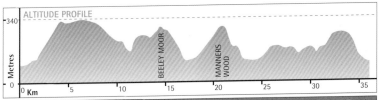

ALTITUDE PROFILE

Metres — 340 — 0

0 Km   5   10   15   20   25   30   35

BEELEY MOOR

MANNERS WOOD

FIVE DALES CIRCUIT   GRADE: ▲

TOTAL DISTANCE: 36KM » **TOTAL ASCENT:** 1,074M » **TIME:** 3 HRS+ » **START/FINISH:** DARLEY BRIDGE
START GRID REF: SK 270620 » **SATNAV:** DE4 2JY » **PARKING:** DARLEY BRIDGE FREE CAR PARK » **OS MAP:** EXPLORER OL24
THE PEAK DISTRICT – WHITE PEAK AREA » **PUB:** THREE STAGS HEADS, DARLEY BRIDGE TEL: 01629 734 871
CAFÉ: BRING SANDWICHES.

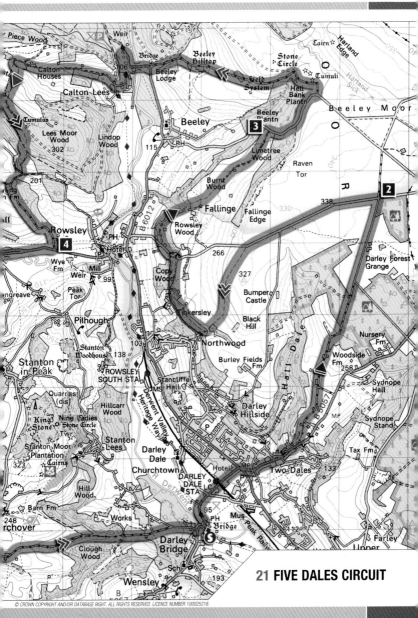

21 FIVE DALES CIRCUIT

Directions – Five Dales Circuit

↱ Turn **R** out of the car park along the B5057 for 800m. Cross the A6 and then continue for 800m on the same B road to the start of the climb. Steep hairpins lead to a row of terraced cottages; turn **L** after the last house up the rough and tough track, joining Flash Lane to a crossroads.

2 Turn **L** onto the road to the brow of the Rowsley Bar climb, then **L** through double gates onto a bridleway. Descend on the obvious track, then keep **R** along the contouring woodland bridleway, passing through the two gates where the track intersects. At the road, descend via two hairpins and take the farm track **R** just after the house. Climb for 200m until the bridleway drops **L** into woods, then climbs sharply to a wooden bridge. Turn **sharp R** after the bridge and climb via gates into fields, and take the farm track between buildings heading **NE** to join the main road.

3 Turn **R** onto Beeley Hill for 1km, then **L** at the right-hand bend and take the obvious rough track downhill to Chatsworth Road. Keep **R** and go over the bridge, following signs for the car park. Go through this to a gate and, after the houses, head **NW** up the track for 1.5km, zigzagging through farm buildings to a gate. Go **L** through a gate up the wall edge, through the next gate and climb up to Manners Wood. At the top, pass through the double gates and onto the obvious path through the woods. Turn **L** at the junction after the first steep section and immediately **R** down the next. At the crossroads, go **SA** then **L** at the junction, over a slight rise and down fast bends to the main road.

4 Turn **R** onto the A6 for 2km until Haddon Hall car park. Take the bridleway **L** just beyond the car park, climb along the obvious track then wall and fence edge, through bridlegate by farm building and **SA** along fence. Turn **L** through gate and follow steep path down technical hairpins to pond, then continue **SA** up small lane towards Youlgreave church. **SA** at crossroads. Keep **L** at next downhill junction, watch out for bridleway hidden on the **L** behind parked cars on left when road bends right. Drop to cross footbridge, then **L** along river for 150m and follow lane uphill to **R**. Bear off **R** after farmhouse alongside rickety caravans, and take track across fields, across small lane, then obvious track down to river and up other side to B5056.

5 Turn **R** onto the road then **L** up minor road signposted *Birchover*. Climb through the village, and just after village shop, turn **R** down lane. At brow of hill (250m, village stocks opposite), take track **L** and continue until bottom of steep rutted track. Keep **R** then immediately **L** and drop down potholed tarmac lane to join road – keep **R** downhill to Darley Bridge. Turn **L** at junction, over bridge to return to the start.

◄⚙◦ Making a day of it

At 36km this is already a big ride. But if it's not enough, the kilometre just after Calton Lees Farm is shared with the Bakewell Circuit (see page 25). Lap this as many times as you feel necessary before continuing.

NORTHWOOD

22 Linacre Classic

Introduction

A good-length ride that takes in most of what is great about the eastern side of the White Peak. There's singletrack galore, the price paid being the stretches of lane that link it all together. It's worth it though. Trails like the drop from Cartledge to Brindwoodgate, the sinuous moorland trail of Harewood Moor, the descent from Wigley and the Shillito singletrack are all crackers, and that's just the downs ... Rising and falling throughout its length, with plenty of pedalling, it gives a compelling case for bringing the light bike and the circus wheels. Fit lads (and lasses) will fly round this one. Note that things can get overgrown mid-summer, so it's a good ride to save for a dry spring or late summer day.

The Ride

The early climb from Linacre reservoirs warms the legs before the fun descent from Old Brampton. Road graft to Holymoorside is followed by off-road graft before the short-lived descent that precedes the sadly-resurfaced Hungerhill Lane (used to be a cracking descent, this, in reverse). Billy Big Legs on his Billy Big Wheels should impressively smoke this climb. The wonderful singletrack over Harewood Moor never gets old, and then we're linking over to Wigley before the fun kicks in again. A great descent, a tough climb and more ups, downs and lanes round to Shillito woods and the fun singletrack round that way. More off- and on-road climbing before three fun descents. The first from Horsleygate Lane is merely a warm-up for the zoom down from Cartledge. The Gateland Lane singletrack rounds things off before a bit more graft back to the start.

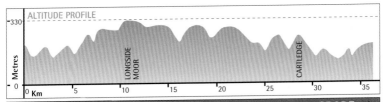

LINACRE CLASSIC | GRADE: ▲

TOTAL DISTANCE: 35KM » **TOTAL ASCENT:** 1,050M » **TIME:** 2.5-4 HRS » **START/FINISH:** LINACRE RESERVOIRS, OFF THE B6050
START GRID REF: SK 334729 » **SATNAV:** S42 7JW » **PARKING:** PAY AND DISPLAY, LINACRE RESERVOIRS
OS MAP: EXPLORER OL24 THE PEAK DISTRICT – WHITE PEAK AREA » **PUB:** THE PEACOCK INN, CUTTHORPE TEL: 01246 232 834
CAFÉ: ICE CREAM VAN AT THE CAR PARK ON NICE DAYS.

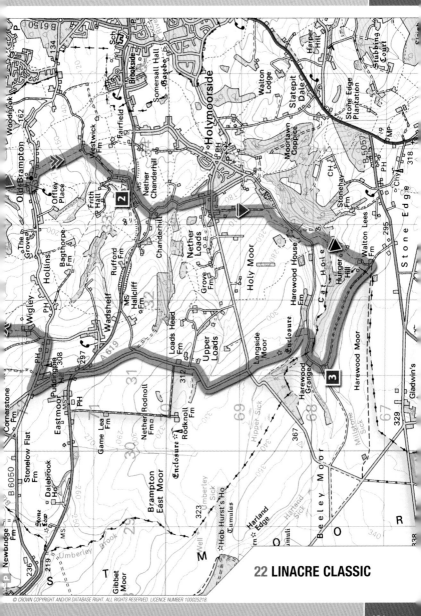

22 LINACRE CLASSIC

Directions — Linacre Classic

➎ Park in the first car park at Linacre and turn **R** down the road into the woods, passing the toilets and ranger centre, onto a wide gravel trail. Cross a wide bridge and turn **R** (unsigned) onto a trail uphill along the edge of the woods. Turns to singletrack and climbs to Old Brampton. Turn **L** on the road, and then **R** after 200m onto a fun singletrack bridleway descent. Turn **R** at the track junction and climb to the A619 road.

2 Cross the road with care and turn almost immediately **L** onto Chandler Hill Lane. Keep **L** at junction after 400m and descend road to Holymoorside. Turn **R** at junction with Loads Lane and climb for 300m. Turn **L** onto marked singletrack bridleway. Climbs for a while and eventually turns to fun, though short-lived, descent. Turn **R** at road. Turn **L** after 250m onto signed byway (Hungerhill Lane). Descent followed by steep, tough gravel climb. Keep **R** at track junction and climb to Walton Lees Farm. Turn **R** onto signed bridleway. Doubletrack gives way to fine singletrack over Harewood Moor. At far side pass through double gates and turn **R** to meet the road.

3 Turn **R** on road for 500m and then turn **L** through gate onto signed bridleway climb. Bears **L** and over Longside Moor (usually past loads of cows) to a gate at the far side of the field and the road. **SA** onto the road and follow it to the A619. Cross road with care onto minor road opposite. Turn **R** at junction, climb and descend. Turn **L** just after pub onto dead end road. Keep **R** towards Wigley and keep an eye out for **easy-to-miss** bridleway on the **L** next to a stone toadstool. Fun descent to the stream, followed by tough singletrack climb to Birley Farm. Watch for gate **R** of the drive and cross the field. Turn **R** onto the drive, then **R** again through a gate onto singletrack after the stream. Turns to farm drive. Climb to road.

4 Turn **L** at road, then bear **R** onto second road, on the bend. Turn **R** after 600m towards Grange Lumb Farm (heed the *Slow Down* signs!). Pass to the **L** of the farm and through woods to Grangewood Farm. Climb to road. Turn **L*** on road for just under 2km. After woods on right, look for bridleway **SA** through gate at lane junction. Take this. Follow central line, avoiding left or right options. Splash through stream after 1.5km and turn **R** down track. Turns to tarmac and climbs to T-junction. Turn **L** and descend to road. **R** at road and then turn **L** onto signed bridleway, immediately after road on right signed *Unthank*.

OR *Shortly after joining the road turn **R** onto signed byway (Johnnygate Lane). Fun descent. **SA** at tarmac, then **L** at farm (watch your speed!) onto narrow signed byway. Continue to Millthorpe. Turn **L** onto main road and ride for approx. 800m. Turn **R** onto signed bridleway immediately before left turn signed *Unthank*.

5 (Optional Route rejoins here.) Climb to road (Horsleygate Lane), turn **R** and continue climbing for approx. 900m. Turn **R** onto signed bridleway between houses (sign partially hidden in bushes). Descend gravelly trail through gates. Upon rejoining the road, turn **L** and climb for approx. 1km to Cartledge. Turn **R** onto lane at top, turns to bridleway. Great descent, but **take care** as it's a popular trail with other users.

6 Turn **L** at the bottom, keep **L** at the junction and climb for 300m. Turn **R** onto track signed *Unsuitable for Motor Vehicles* and climb to road. Turn **R**. After 800m turn **R** onto signed bridleway as road bends left. Keep **SA** to meet tarmac. Continue **SA** and bear **L** onto main road. Turn **R** after 400m up Wilkin Hill and then **L** after 300m onto a bridleway. Drop and climb to Common Lane and turn **L** (**SA**) into Cutthorpe. Turn **R** on the main road, and then **L** after 1.2km back to the reservoir car park.

23 Hope Valley Circuit

Introduction

Strictly speaking this is mostly on the Dark Peak map, but it's included here as a good proportion of the route is on the 'white stuff'. This is basically a really big loop around the Hope Valley, taking in several tough climbs and some fantastic descents.

The Ride

Several starting points are possible, but Hathersage is our favourite, although that does leave the toughest climb until last. Out of the village, height is quickly gained on a quiet lane, then steady singletrack leads up onto the limestone, before a great descent to Bradwell, and a proper long slog up onto the moors above Castleton. Maintaining height, the route swings north towards and then over Mam Tor, before heading back east for the long return leg. Great descending and ascending into and back out of Edale, takes in some of the best riding the Dark Peak has to offer. A descent from Win Hill brings you back into the Hope Valley. A quick blast drops the tiring rider into Bamford, from where a mean little lane climbs up to the edge of Stanage Moor and the Long Causeway climb up to Stanage Edge. The descent is superb, and technical in places, before a finale down the lane back to Hathersage.

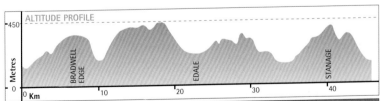

ALTITUDE PROFILE

450

Metres

BRADWELL EDGE

EDALE

STANAGE

0 Km   10   20   30   40

HOPE VALLEY CIRCUIT   **GRADE: ▲»▲**

TOTAL DISTANCE: 45KM » **TOTAL ASCENT**: 1,529M » **TIME**: 4–6 HRS » **START/FINISH**: HATHERSAGE
START GRID REF: SK 231814 » **SATNAV**: S32 1DU » **PARKING**: HATHERSAGE PAY AND DISPLAY
OS MAP: EXPLORER OL1 THE PEAK DISTRICT – DARK PEAK AREA » **PUB**: PLENTY TO CHOOSE FROM IN HATHERSAGE
CAFÉ: OUTSIDE CAFE TEL: 01433 651 936; HATHERSAGE POOL CAFÉ TEL: 01433 651 159.

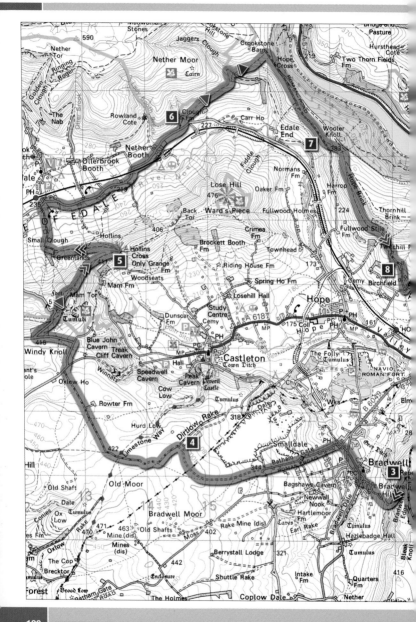

23 HOPE VALLEY CIRCUIT

Directions – Hope Valley Circuit

↪ Turn **R** out of Hathersage car park, then **L** downhill on the B6001 towards Grindleford. Just after 1km take the tarmac road **R** signed *Gliding Club/Abney*. Climb the road for 1.4km branching **R** on the narrow tarmac road just before the farm complex of Highlow Hall on the brow. Follow the narrow road through trees, traversing around the valley head, past Callow House. Just before Offerton Hall, at the right-hand bend in the descending lane, go **SA** on the bridleway across moorland. The trail climbs steadily before a short descent to a gate and junction with the road.

2 Turn **L** up the road and track past the mast and along the level rutted track onto Shatton Moor. At a vague T-junction keep **L** on bridleway following track as it curves round **R** passing a footpath coming in from the left. Pass roadhead on left, keep **SA** and descend fast, looking out for a bridleway signed through gate on **L**. If the track gets steep you've missed the bridleway sign.

3 Take this bridleway across the field and then **L** downhill, on singletrack – superb – eventually emerging in the village of Bradwell. Go **R** on main road, through traffic lights, then turn **L** onto Town Lane, just before the football playing field. Up to the junction, ignore bridleway signed straight ahead, turn **L**, and keep **SA** uphill out of the village. Turn **R** at the T-junction, and follow the road as it starts to curve round.

4 **SA** onto a rough quarry track, before the road starts to descend again. Follow this for a few metres, turning **L** up the stony lane of Dirtlow Rake. Keep **SA**, past various old quarries, to a gate. **SA**, keep **SA** at the junction of bridleways (right goes off to the awesome descent of Cave Dale into Castleton), then take the byway **R** at the next junction. Follow this **SA** to reach the main road. Turn **R** and follow the road round, ignoring right turns to Winnats Pass and Blue John Cavern. Take the next road **R** up to Mam Nick, just after the large car park on the right. Just over the brow, at a bus stop, go through the gate and **R** on the singletrack along the side of Mam Tor (not the one to the left which descends), climbing initially then descending to the cairn at Hollins Cross.

5 Turn back sharp **L**, and take the excellent fast and sweeping descent, eventually meeting the lane coming up from Edale. Turn **R** onto this lane, and follow it down to the main valley road. Turn **R** and head down the valley. After passing the Youth Hostel and riding school, look out for a gate on the **L**, and bridleway entrance, signed *Footpath and Bridleway to Alport*.

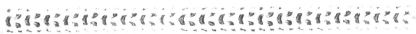

6 Go through the gate, **SA** up walled path. Cross the ford, through the gate and **SA** up a pleasant track through two further gates before **SA** for the steep descent to Jaggers Clough – get into low gear before ford and gate. Cross ford through gate and **SA** up steep and loose track. **SA** to junction with Roman road. Turn **R**, through gate and down the track.

7 At a gate ignore stony track descending **R**, but take the singletrack and ruts climbing to the **L** beside the woods, uphill onto the broad shoulder of Win Hill. Keep **SA** for about 500m, looking out for a small cairn on the **R** (don't keep following the track – if you get to a gate you've missed the cairn). Take the narrow trail off to the **R**, a fast descent down the flank of Win Hill. Go **SA** through the gate, up to a second gate and **SA** across the field, picking up a prominent track – the muddy lane, down through a couple of gates, to emerge onto tarmac at Edge Farm.

8 Drop down the lane and turn **L** at the T-junction. Keep **SA** through the village of Aston and along the narrow road to Thornhill. Turn **R** in the village, down to the main Hope Valley road. Turn **L** and head up to the traffic lights at Sickleholme Service Station. Turn **L**, over the railway bridge, and take the first **R**, up Saltergate Lane. Turn **R** at the top, and head **SA** along the *Unsuitable for Motors* Hurst Clough Lane. Ignore left branch at single bar gate to sewage works, keep **SA** and descend into Hurst Clough, get in low gear (you have been warned) for a shocking climb out on those tiring legs. Keep **SA** on lane, up past the farms and eventually onto the road. Turn **L**.

9 Head up the lane. Keep **SA** onto the track, just past the cattle-grid and small parking area, up the ever steepening Long Causeway. At the summit, follow the track onto the moor, and where the track bears left heading out across to Stanage Pole, turn **R** back down to the edge. Head back on yourself for a few metres and start the descent, with a few very tricky little steps, twists and turns. The trail continues its superb technical descending, requiring concentration throughout. After the second gate, just after emerging from the trees, branch off to the **L**, across the grass and down to the road.

10 Turn **L**, and **L** again at the junction, uphill. Turn **R** at the top, over the cattle grid and onto a rapid tarmac descent back into Hathersage. Turn **R** onto the main road, then **L** and **L** again into the car park. Well done!

CHATSWORTH

24 Rowsley Circuit

Introduction

Another big old circle of mountain biking fun. Centred in the heart of the White Peak, it has plenty of ups and downs, lots of singletrack and, while challenging, is a good introduction to longer routes, especially when the trails are dry. Highlights are too numerous to mention, but this is a great summer ride and a fun one to do with a bunch of friends.

The Ride

From Rowsley steady climbing gives way to tough climbing on fantastic trails leading onto the Duke of Devonshire's front garden. From the village of Edensor the route climbs up and then descends with speed and fun down to Bakewell, crosses the Wye and heads over the farmland pastures of Haddon to a delightful, skill-testing descent to Lathkill Dale. Passing through the villages of Youlgreave and Birchover, on great, varied terrain, the final descent, after a chunk of climbing out of Darley Dale, is a fitting finale to this fine ride.

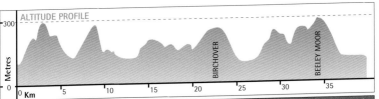

ROWSLEY CIRCUIT   **GRADE:** ▲

TOTAL DISTANCE: 38.5KM » **TOTAL ASCENT:** 1,170M » **TIME:** 3 HRS+ » **START/FINISH:** ROWSLEY
START GRID REF: SK 257659 » **SATNAV:** DE4 2EL » **PARKING:** ROWSLEY CAR PARK » **OS MAP:** EXPLORER OL24
THE PEAK DISTRICT – WHITE PEAK AREA » **PUB:** THE FARMYARD INN, YOULGREAVE TEL: 01629 636 211; DEVONSHIRE ARMS,
BEELEY TEL: 01629 733 259 » **CAFÉ:** LOADS IN BAKEWELL.

24 ROWSLEY CIRCUIT

Directions – Rowsley Circuit

 From the car park, head west on the A6 (towards Bakewell) for a short distance, before taking the first **R**, up Church Lane. Follow this **SA** to where it gives up its tarmac and heads off into the Peak, traversing through woodland, to reach a crossroads. Ignore the tracks off to the left and straight ahead, but go through the gate on the **R** and up the dirt singletrack into the woods. Superb hard, but rideable climbing through the trees. You emerge onto a level piece of track, but after a short few metres, breath recovered, branch off **R** uphill once again. The track levels off, onto fast woodland singletrack which twists and turns to a gate.

2 Go through the double gates and downhill, fast and furious, to the woods and another gate. Go **R** down the trail (not straight ahead) and fork **L** where the bridleway splits. Follow the track up across the field and into the woods. **SA** through the woods. Where the track emerges, go **SA** down the parkland – watch those jumps! Aim for a small clump of trees, fingerposts mark the way. Turn **R** just before the trees and keep going across the Devonshires' front lawn towards the road.

3 Turn **L** down the road, soon branching off to the **L** onto a signed bridleway which cuts the corner, back onto the road, then **L** signed *Edensor Tea Rooms*. Continue **SA** keeping the church to your left. Up the road, then track – a good honest climb. Ride **SA** on the road at the top. Just beyond the brow of the hill, and immediately after a farm track on the left and before Ballcross Farm on the right, take the bridleway steeply down into the trees. Superb classic MTB descending brings one to the golf course. Cross this (danger – imagine the embarrassment of being hit). Drop onto the Monsal Trail, heading **L** (south), to where it ends. Turn off the trail, ignore the tarmac and drop down into the fields towards the river. Follow the bridleway as it weaves along the valley floor, before exiting onto a metalled road.

4 Turn **R** and follow the road onto the main A6. Turn **R** and head along the busy road for 750m to the edge of Bakewell. Take the lane off to the **L** – Intake Lane. Follow this deteriorating into a field to soon meet another road. Turn **L** and, after 500m, at the bend in the road, go **SA** through the gate onto the farm track. Follow the track towards farm buildings. Just before the buildings, turn **R**, through the gate, along the side of the field. Turn **L** through a gate and follow a steep path down hairpins to a pond, then continue **SA** up the small lane and keep **L** towards Youlgreave church.

5 Ride **SA** at the crossroads in the village, keep **L** at the next downhill junction, and watch out for a bridleway hidden behind parked cars on the **L** when the road bends right. Drop to cross the footbridge, then turn **L** along the river for 150m and follow the lane uphill to the **R**. Bear **R** after the farmhouse alongside rickety caravans, and take the track across fields, across a small lane, another field and then down an obvious track to the river and up the other side to the B5056. Turn **R** onto the road then **L** up minor road signposted *Birchover*.

6 Climb through the village, and just after the village shop on your left turn **R** down a lane. At the brow of the hill (250m, village stocks opposite), take the track **L** and continue until the bottom of a steep rutted track. Keep **R** then immediately **L** and drop down potholed tarmac lane to join road – keep **R** downhill to Darley Bridge. Turn **L** at the T-junction and follow the road, crossing the river. Take the first **L**, 300m after the bridge. Follow this road to where it joins the A6.

7 Turn **R** on the A6 then first **L** climbing out of the valley. Keep on this road, ignoring three minor roads off to the right, take the fourth **R**, Lumb Lane, that being the small lane to the **R**, 100m before the road turns left and starts to descend again. Follow this lane, turning up **R** onto the bridleway before the corner. Head uphill, looking out for the bridleway off to the **L** just before the edge of the woods. Follow this contouring bridleway through woods, passing through two gates where a track intersects. At the road, descend via two hairpins and take the farm track **R** just after house. Climb for 200m until the bridleway drops **L** into woods, then climbs sharply to a wooden bridge. Turn sharp **R** after the bridge and climb via a gate into fields, taking the farm track between buildings heading **NE**. Join road after 1.5km, turn **R** onto Beeley Hill for 1km, then keep **L** on right-hand bend and take obvious rough track downhill to Chatsworth Road.

8 Turn **L** and follow the road (B6012) back to Rowsley.

◄◻◻◻ **Making a day of it**

One for the rock climbers out there – this route circles Stanton Moor (GR SK 244629), runs right by Rowtor Rocks (roughly GR SK 235621) and isn't a million miles away from Robin Hood's Stride and Cratcliffe (again, roughly GR SK 227623) – two of our favourite places in the Peak. Our *Peak District Bouldering* guide includes them all, as do our *Day Walks in the Peak District* walking guidebooks.

SECTION 4

Bonus Section

Done all the rides? Day and night, winter and summer? Linked them all together? Traversed the Peak north to south, east to west? Well what more can we offer? I'm afraid it's either taking the kids out on one of our family rides or forgetting about being able to have kids, and tackling the Hollinsclough descents.

TENTERHILL DESCENT FROM BOOTH FARM

Hollinsclough Descents

⚠ **Warning** Serious Hardcore Descents

While the Peak is overflowing with good hills to throw yourself down, there is perhaps no greater concentration of seriously hardcore, technical descents than around the village of Hollinsclough in the White Peak. There are several fast downhills, but the character of these bad boys is more intensive, big drop, rock steps. Armour is probably a good idea.

1 Tenterhill from Golling Gate
A do-able rock step descent to the ford over the River Dove – good stuff.

2 Tenterhill from Booth Farm
Can be ridden fast, steepening all the time to the ford on the Dove – easy stuff.

3 Hollinsclough Rake
Singletrack with a mega finish down to the ford.

4 Hollinsclough Moor to Hollinsclough
Two routes down, both very hardcore, with perhaps the route down from Coatestown being the Big Daddy.
5

HOLLINSCLOUGH DESCENTS   GRADE: ▲»▲

START/FINISH: HOLLINSCLOUGH, FROM WHERE ALL THE HILLS ARE A SHORT RIDE AWAY
START GRID REF: SK 066666 (YES REALLY!) » **PARKING**: LIMITED PARKING IN THE VILLAGE » **PUB**: THE QUIET WOMAN, EARL STERNDALE TEL: 01298 83211 » **CAFÉ**: BRING SANDWICHES, OR LONGNOR NOT FAR AWAY.

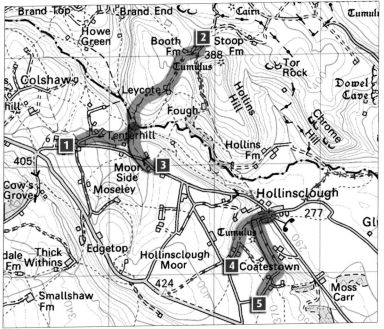

DESCENDING INTO CHEEDALE PHOTO: TIM RUSSON

The Pennine Bridleway

Introduction

More rugged and wild than some of the other trails described here, the full Pennine Bridleway would take around two weeks to ride (there's a challenge if ever I heard one). Fully signposted throughout its length, the Pennine Bridleway is the first purpose-built long-distance bridleway in Britain, linking the High Peak Trail in Derbyshire to Cumbria, near Kirkby Stephen. The idea was initially conceived by Lady Mary Towneley, a keen horse rider, who campaigned for a long-distance route over the Pennines for riders for many years until her death in February 2001.

The Ride

Beginning on the High Peak Trail near Matlock, it follows the old Cromford and High Peak Railway through the limestone valleys of the White Peak and then turns up onto the Packhorse Road – the first of many packhorse trails along the way – which it follows from Tideswell across the moorland of the Dark Peak to Hayfield. Leaving Derbyshire, it picks its way between moors and reservoirs as it runs north to meet the 75.6km Mary Towneley Loop in Lancashire and a 16km loop near Settle in North Yorkshire. The former loop is a popular ride in its own right and a tough challenge to complete in a day. Leaving the loop, the trail heads on to reach its conclusion at the edge of the Howgill Fells in Cumbria.

THE PENNINE BRIDLEWAY

TOTAL DISTANCE: UP TO AROUND 330KM EACH WAY (!) » **MAP**: HARVEY PENNINE BRIDLEWAY ROUTE MAP
WEBSITE: WWW.NATIONALTRAIL.CO.UK/PENNINEBRIDLEWAY.

Family Rides

Introduction

Hills, rocks and children don't always mix. Kids might have a real affinity for mud, but on the whole, the majority of the routes in this book probably aren't the sort of rides you might take your family on. So, if you've decided, in the spirit of self-sacrifice, that your day's riding will be spent with the kids, we've included a few rides that are suitable to help you out. Of course, they're also good for an easy day out, or for introducing friends to mountain biking. You can also check out our *Cycling in the Peak District* book for more ideas.

Tissington Trail

The Tissington Trail is a well-known route that follows the tracks of a disused railway line. As with the High Peak Trail, there is a gentle drop as the trail runs south; nothing too severe but a possible consideration when planning a ride. (Tackle the hill with fresh legs from the south and kids will have forgotten all about the climb by the time they've free-wheeled most of the way back to the car!) The former railway was the Ashbourne to Buxton line, completed in 1899 and closed in 1967. Four years later it then became one of the first lines to be re-opened as a recreational trail.

The Tissington Trail meets both the High Peak Trail and the Pennine Bridleway at Parsley Hay, so there's nothing stopping you linking them. A technically easy but long ride starts at Ashbourne, climbs the Tissington Trail to Parsley Hay and then drops down the High Peak Trail until it hits the B5056, which it then follows back into Ashbourne.

TISSINGTON TRAIL

DISTANCE: UP TO 21KM EACH WAY ALONG A DISUSED RAILWAY » **OS MAP**: EXPLORER OL24 THE PEAK DISTRICT – WHITE PEAK AREA; LANDRANGER 119 BUXTON & MATLOCK » **START/FINISH**: ASHBOURNE CYCLE HIRE; PARSLEY HAY **START GRID REF**: ASHBOURNE CYCLE HIRE – SK 175469; PARSLEY HAY – SK 147637 » **PARKING**: PAY AND DISPLAY CAR PARK AT PARSLEY HAY; ASHBOURNE » **CYCLE HIRE**: ASHBOURNE CYCLE HIRE TEL: 01335 343156; PARSLEY HAY TEL: 01298 84493 **VISITOR CENTRES**: PARSLEY HAY TEL: 01298 84493; ASHBOURNE TOURIST INFORMATION TEL: 01335 343666.

High Peak Trail

Another well-known route, the High Peak Trail follows the course of the old Cromford and High Peak Railway which, when completed in 1830, was among the earliest in the country. It runs from Parsley Hay at its north end down to Cromford Canal in the south, and is probably most easily ridden as a 'there-and-back' route. It's worth pointing out that the trail does literally run down from north to south, with the steepest sections at the southern end and you should bear this in mind when deciding how far along the route you wish to ride. Unlike many railway routes, the High Peak Trail twists and turns surprisingly sharply as it runs through the limestone scenery of the White Peak, so the views change regularly. Back at Parsley Hay, the trail meets the Tissington Trail, so you can always head off down this if you're still feeling lively.

Middleton Top, about two-thirds of the way down the trail, sits at the top of the Middleton incline and houses a steam winding engine, built in 1892, to haul wagons up and down the incline. It can be seen running on the first weekend of each month in the summer and on bank holidays. Further south, near to High Peak Junction, is the Cromford Canal, where several remnants of the area's historical importance as an industrial centre are still maintained as part of the Derwent Valley Mills World Heritage Site.

HIGH PEAK TRAIL

DISTANCE: UP TO 28KM EACH WAY ALONG A DISUSED RAILWAY PATH » **OS MAP**: EXPLORER OL24 THE PEAK DISTRICT – WHITE PEAK AREA » **START/FINISH:** THIS TRAIL CAN BE STARTED FROM THE NORTH AT PARSLEY HAY, THE HIGH PEAK JUNCTION IN THE SOUTH OR MIDDLETON TOP VISITOR CENTRE, ABOUT TWO THIRDS OF THE WAY DOWN THE TRAIL
START GRID REF: PARSLEY HAY – SK 147637, HIGH PEAK JUNCTION – SK 315561, MIDDLETON TOP – SK 275551
PARKING: PAY AND DISPLAY CAR PARK AT PARSLEY HAY; PARKING ALSO AVAILABLE AT MIDDLETON TOP AND HIGH PEAK JUNCTION
CYCLE HIRE: MIDDLETON TOP CYCLE HIRE CENTRE, TEL: 01629 823204; PARSLEY HAY TEL: 01298 84493
VISITOR CENTRES: MIDDLETON TOP VISITOR CENTRE TEL: 01629 823204; PARSLEY HAY TEL: 01298 84493.

Monsal Trail

Following the line of the old Midland Railway through the centre of the Peak District, the full Monsal Trail is around 14km long, and until recently only a short section, about 8km from Bakewell to Monsal Head, was accessible as four large tunnels remained closed for safety reasons. That changed in 2011, and the trail now runs through the stunning Cheedale as far as Blackwell Mill. It's a lovely ride, fairly flat, and you're on your bike and passing through some lovely scenery – the view down Monsal Dale is one of the best in the Peak, and Cheedale is particularly atmospheric as you emerge from the tunnels.

The full railway line was completed in the 1860s, linking Manchester with London. Bakewell station was used to receive coal from remote areas, and to dispatch milk from local farms to the cities. The line was eventually closed just over a century later and bought by the Peak District National Park Authority, who opened it as a cycle trail in 1981. There are various stops and alternative starting points along the way, including Hassop Station and Miller's Dale Station.

MONSAL TRAIL

DISTANCE: UP TO 14KM EACH WAY ALONG A DISUSED RAILWAY PATH » OS MAP: EXPLORER OL24 THE PEAK DISTRICT – WHITE PEAK AREA; A MAP IS AVAILABLE FOR 50P FROM BAKEWELL CYCLE HIRE » START/FINISH: BAKEWELL CYCLE HIRE START GRID REF: SK 223690 » PARKING: BAKEWELL » CYCLE HIRE: BAKEWELL CYCLE HIRE TEL: 01335 348603; HASSOP STATION CYCLE HIRE TEL: 01629 810588 » VISITOR CENTRE: NONE FOR THE TRAIL ITSELF, BUT BAKEWELL HAS A TOURIST INFORMATION CENTRE TEL: 01629 816558.

Carsington Water

A popular little circuit around Britain's ninth largest reservoir, this is a relatively hilly route that should leave most novices feeling as though they've been on a pretty tough ride. Starting from the visitor centre, the trail circles the reservoir, passing through carefully managed woodland and the stone-built village of Hopton, where you can take a break at the local pub if you need it.

Back at the visitor centre, there's a large adventure playground, a designated barbeque area and opportunities to go horse riding, sailing and canoeing. The centre itself houses a permanent exhibition, explaining the role of water in our lives and a cafe and souvenir shop. The site was awarded a 'Forestry Centre of Excellence' for its management of the local woodland, which is home to a wide variety of wildlife, most notably the birds who reside at the reservoir. You can watch them from two purpose-built hides and from the conservation area on the far side of the lake. Don't leave without a look at the Kugel Stone in the centre of the courtyard. This ball of granite weighs over a tonne and sits on a thin layer of water under pressure, allowing you to move it with the touch of your hand.

CARSINGTON WATER

DISTANCE: 13KM CIRCUIT AROUND A RESERVOIR » **OS MAP**: EXPLORER OL24 THE PEAK DISTRICT – WHITE PEAK AREA; A FREE ROUTE MAP IS ALSO AVAILABLE FROM THE VISITOR CENTRE » **START/FINISH:** CARSINGTON WATER VISITOR CENTRE
START GRID REF: SK 241517 » **PARKING:** PAY AND DISPLAY AT THE VISITOR CENTRE
CYCLE HIRE: CARSINGTON WATER VISITOR CENTRE TEL: 01629 540478
VISITOR CENTRE: CARSINGTON WATER TEL: 01629 540696, WWW.CARSINGTONWATER.COM

top 10 Downhills

White Peak descents range from long, wide rocky blasts to tiny sections of woodland singletrack. Here – in no particular order – are a few of the best.

1 Cumberland Clough
GR SK 002692

While the true descent starts a little further on, the full run starts from the road. Ever increasing speeds, fast corners and loose rocks lead to a gate and brief respite. Just around the corner, a jumbled mass of rocks and roots awaits.

2 Brushfield to Monsal Head
GR SK 175717

A big hill, with sustained descending which just keeps getting steeper, with a nasty twist to drop onto the disused railway line.

3 Golf Course Hill, Bakewell
GR SK 228694

Woodland singletrack leads to a dash across the golf course. Getting more technical every year, this is either hard and fast or slippery and rooty, depending on the season. Fore!

4 Black Brook
GR SJ 997647

A rocky strip of chaos in an otherwise beautiful valley. A twisting rut of pedal strikes and awkward corners. Great fun if you like that sort of thing! Shame about the muddy slog out though.

5 Charity Lane
GR SJ 967728

A road on the many maps, this certainly isn't the case on the ground. Wide, open and straight, it's flat-out rocky fun along the edge of the forest. Turn left at the bottom and scare yourself silly on the steep, loose rocks to the Bottom of the Oven.

Wormhill to Monk's Dale
GR SK 122745

Up out of Wormhill, then a great little descent – all rocky fun – leads down to the opening of Monk's Dale. Lots of great descents exist in this area. It is impossible to pick any one out, but dropping into Cheedale at Great Rocks Dale, either from the north or south, and the descent of the Limestone Way to Monk's Dale Farm are all superb.

Haddon to Youlgreave
GR SK 215652

The Alps come to the White Peak! Sort of, anyway. A short-lived series of tight and slippery limestone switchbacks, this will leave you grinning like a cat from Cheshire. There's nothing else for it – book those flights!

Wigley Hill
GR SK 316720

Fast, action-packed, wooded singletrack fun. Ace in the dry and surprisingly good in the wet if you can keep your speed up. Relatively wide, it slips and slithers down to a fast and splashy finish.

Lower Johnnygate
GR SK 319757

Short and unexpected, this narrow, rocky and wet run doesn't leave a lot of room for manoeuvre. Try and find a dry line on the bank or give up and splash down the centre. Great fun either way.

Hollinsclough, the easy one
GR SK 059675

Surrounded by the infamous rocky Tenterhill rubblefests, this is the mild-mannered option around Hollinsclough. Swoopy, grassy and bouncy descending, with a singletrack zigzag down to the brook.

top 10 Climbs

So you think you can climb. On roots?
OK – not too bad? Mud? Slippery limestone?
All three at once? Tick this little lot and we'll
be impressed. Remember – no dabs now ...

1 Monsal Head
GR SK 183718

The daddy of White Peak climbs – steep and long, not technical, just plain hard work. I'd like to say it eases towards the top, but it doesn't. There is ample traction in the dry, which just makes failure more frustrating.

2 Amber Valley Challenge
GR SK 348628

Another tough climb – only for the best. After leaving Ashover, the trail drops to the River Amber, then rears up, steep, hard, only easing off at Overton Hall. You'll probably need specialist climbing tyres, inflated appropriately on a lightweight rig – and a huge set of lungs and legs.

3 Gradbach
GR SJ 990657

Ride the stream at the bottom of this one at your peril – it's covered with slime, making wet feet a virtual certainty. Wet or not, however, the permissive bridleway climb up to Swythamley Hall is great. It's not steep or technical, just a pleasant climb through the woods.

4 Sydnope Hill
GR SK 284632

A big lung buster – hard at the start, especially after rain when the trail gets washed out. Not helped by the steep road start from Darley Dale! Anyway the best will cruise the rocky start and sprint on to the top. The rest of us may need a bit of grit to make it.

5 Three Shire Heads
GR SK 009685

Heading up and around Cut-Thorn Hill, this sand and gritstone climb really belongs in the Dark Peak. Make it through each rock garden and there's always a smooth bit to recover on. Using the banks is cheating.

PHOTO: TIM RUSSON

Johnnygate Lane
GR SK 316755

Usually ridden as a (great) descent, this is an awesome climb. Steep and getting steeper in the middle, the top half has a huge rut running right up the centre. Great fun.

Overton Hall
GR SK 344623

The short but tough section up through the quarry is the challenge here. Slippery in the wet and always steep at the top, it's a toughie. Do it in a oner from the very bottom (or even combined with climb no. 2), hopping the motorbike barriers for an extra challenge.

Holy Moor Hill
GR SK 329682

A good climb. A couple of little technical challenges at the start, but easing all the way. Another of those rare singletrack climbs, with good riding on the descent to Wellspring Farm.

Pilsley Lane
GR SK 234713

A good little challenge. Smooth and well-surfaced, it's the steepness that'll get you on this one!

Intake Road
GR SK 298568

Such a fantastic woodland trail, you'll hardly notice you are going uphill. Steep on the tarmac start, but once in the woods enjoy easy ground, tranquillity and remnants of the industrial revolution.

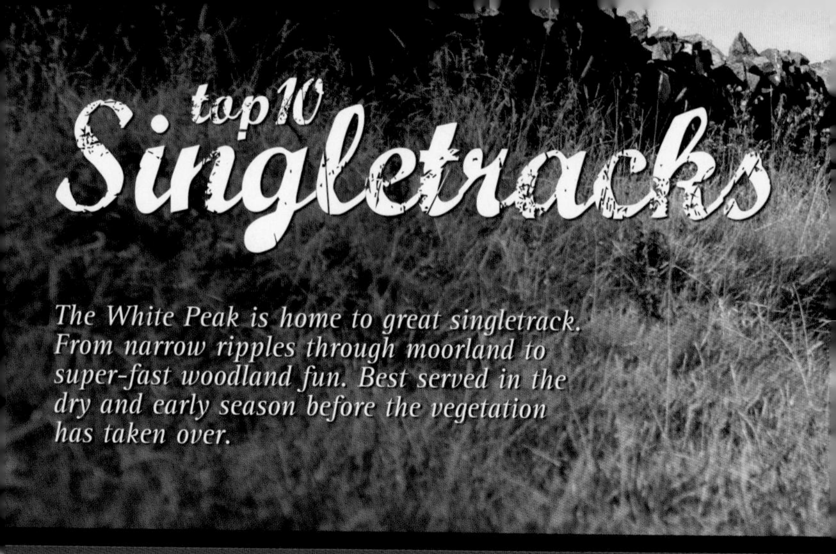

top 10 Singletracks

The White Peak is home to great singletrack. From narrow ripples through moorland to super-fast woodland fun. Best served in the dry and early season before the vegetation has taken over.

1 Cartledge

GR SK 324771

Smooth dirt through a tunnel of trees that lasts forever, this is one of the best singletrack descents in the Peak District. It's only slightly marred by the blind corners which, although brilliant fun, do mean that a previously unseen horse's backside could be only a few metres away.

2 Kelstedge

GR SK 325637

Starting from a posh driveway, this sublime singletrack descent soon deteriorates into a gully full of rocks, drops, twists, turns and undergrowth. Sketchy at times, straightforward at others, it's a great way to get down a hill. A couple of bridges at the bottom present the opportunity to test your trials skills too ...

3 Cockerspring Wood (aka the Ashover Gully Run)

GR SK 347623

A fantastic, relatively-straightforward, swoopy, tree-lined, gully run. Watch out for the log halfway down, which periodically rolls across the track. Fast fun.

4 Harewood Moor

GR SK 311677

The Dark Peak comes south! A superbly unexpected stretch of pristine moorland singletrack, snaking across the heath. Best ridden east to west, but a blast either way.

5 Northwood

GR SK 270648

Best ridden by coming in, downhill, across the fields and then turning north to Beeley Moor, this woodland singletrack is fast and usually covered in leaves – making the frequent rocky water-crossings rather more interesting than you might like!

Baslow Edge

GR SK 258740

Quite technical, and in a great setting, the trail drops down from the edge, and then picks its way back towards the road. Lots of blocks, streams and bomb-holes to navigate.

Bradwell Edge

GR SK 182810

Dropping off the White Peak's limestone plateau into the heart of the Hope Valley, this great trail turns sharp left out of grassy fields and into a narrow and tree-lined trench. Dodging sharp-edged gritstone blocks, it suddenly swings right, widens and plunges steeply downhill to a gate. As this final plummet is over frequently-wet and grip-less mud, stopping can be an issue ...

Manners Wood

GR SK 242679

Around the Chatsworth estate are a lot of great woodland trails, which we can't ride. This one, however, we can, and it's great. Flat and pedally, then steep and fast, then catch-a-pedal-rocky, it's great fun, if a little short.

Coombs Dale – Bleaklow

GR SK 212739

A pleasant cruise through fields of short, dusty grass. Worth riding for the views alone.

Long Dale

GR SK 205592

A great little descent into a fine dry valley and a pleasant blast along the trail leads to a steady climb out, all on quintessential mountain bike trails.

Appendix

Tourist Information Centres
www.visitpeakdistrict.com

Bakewell .... T: 01629 813 227

Buxton .... T: 01298 251 06

Castleton .... T: 01629 816 572

Macclesfield .... T: 01625 378 123

Matlock .... T: 01629 761 103

Bike Shops
This is just a selection – there are loads more in the surrounding towns and cities.

18Bikes
Hope .... T: 01433 621 111

Mark Anthony Cycles/Activesport
Buxton .... T: 01298 22002

Stanley Fearns Cycles
Matlock .... T: 01629 582 089

The Bike Factory
Whaley Bridge .... T: 01663 735 020

Sett Valley Cycles
New Mills .... T: 01663 742 629

Bike Hire
Carsington Water
Visitor Centre .... T: 01629 540 478

Middleton Top
Cycle Hire Centre .... T: 01629 823 204

Parsley Hay Cycle Hire Centre ... T: 01298 84 493

Hassop Station Cycle Hire ..... T: 01629 810 588

Food and Drink
Just a small selection of the many places to eat and drink in the Peak.

Cafes
Woodbine Cafe
Hope .... T: 07778 113 882

Outside Cafe
Hathersage .... T: 01433 651 936

The Bakewell Pudding Parlour ... T: 01629 815 107

Pubs
Bull's Head
Monyash .... T: 01629 812 372

The Druid Inn
Birchover .... T: 01629 653 836

The Red Lion
Litton .... T: 01298 871 458

The Quiet Woman
Earl Sterndale .... T: 01298 83 211

Three Stags Heads
Wardlow Mires .... T: 01298 872 268

Old Sun Inn
Buxton .... T: 01298 23 452

The Monsal Head Hotel
Monsal Head .... T: 01629 640 250

The Grouse Inn
Froggatt .... T: 01433 630 423

Weather
www.metoffice.gov.uk

www.bbc.co.uk/weather

Accommodation
It's beyond the remit of this guide to give you a full run-down of tourist accommodation in the Peak. Here are a few places that have been recommended to us, but, being local, we haven't always had direct experience of them ourselves.

YHA Hostels
Youlgreave .... T: 0870 371 9151

Hathersage .... T: 0845 371 9021

Hartington Hall .... T: 0845 371 9740

Go to: www.yha.org.uk for more information.

Hotels, Self Catering & B&B
There are millions to choose from. Your best option is to look on:

www.peakdistrictonline.co.uk, or

www.peakdistrict-nationalpark.com

The Woodbine Cafe and B&B..T: 07778 113 882

Campsites

North Lees
Hathersage .... T: 01433 650 838

Eric Byne
Baslow .... T: 01246 582 277

Other Publications

Peak District Mountain Biking – Dark Peak Trails
Jon Barton, Vertebrate Publishing
www.v-publishing.co.uk

**Cycling in the Peak District –
Off-Road Trails & Quiet Lanes**
Jon Barton & Tom Fenton, Vertebrate Publishing
www.v-publishing.co.uk

**Great Britain Mountain Biking – The Best Trail
Riding in England, Scotland and Wales**
Tom Fenton & Andy McCandlish, Vertebrate Publishing
www.v-publishing.co.uk

About the Author

Jon found that living on the confluence of his Dark
Peak and White Peak guides simply too tempting
and has now retreated back to the city, taking wife,
child, and – surprisingly – long lived dog with him.
Sheffield does at least have the advantage of every
ride finishing with a descent through Blacka. Climbing
or riding every week in the Peak remains the ideal in
his life, but recently dark forces have been at work,
and once or twice he's been spotted wearing shorts
and trainers, notebook in hand, perhaps working to
complete the set; authoring walking, biking, climbing
and now a running guide. Dark rumours.

Vertebrate Publishing

Mountain Bike Rider (MBR) Magazine called our
MTB guides '...a series of glossy, highly polished
and well researched guidebooks to some of the
UK's favourite riding spots.'

We want to provide you – the rider – with well-
researched, informative, functional, inspirational
and great-looking MTB guide-books that document
the superb riding across the length and breadth
of the UK. So if you want to go riding somewhere,
you can always count on us to point you in the
right direction.

As well as our series of MTB guidebooks, we have
award-winning and bestselling titles covering a
range of leisure activities, including; cycling, rock
climbing, hillwalking and others. We are best
known for our MTB titles, including the bestseller
Dark Peak Mountain Biking, which BIKEmagic.com
said was 'far and away the best Peak guide we've
come across'.

Our autobiography of the British rock climbing
legend **Jerry Moffatt** won the *Grand Prize* at the
2009 Banff Mountain Book Festival.

We also produce many leading outdoor titles for
other publishers including the Mountain Training
UK (MTUK) and rock climbing guidebooks for the
British Mountaineering Council and the Fell and
Rock Climbing Club. For more information, please
visit our website: **www.v-publishing.co.uk** or
email us: **info@v-publishing.co.uk**

MOUNTAIN BIKING GUIDEBOOKS

About the Great Outdoors

The great outdoors is not bottom bracket friendly; beautiful flowing singletrack can give way suddenly to scary rock gardens, hard climbs can appear right at the end of a ride and sheep will laugh at your attempts to clean your nemesis descent. Of course it's not all good news. You'll need a good bike to ride many of the routes in our set of mountain biking guides. You'll also need fuel, spare clothing, first aid skills, endurance, power, determination and plenty of nerve.

Bridleways litter our great outdoors. Our guides, written by local riders, reveal the secrets of their local area's best rides from 6 to 300km in length, including ideas for link-ups and night-riding options. Critically acclaimed, our comprehensive series of guides is the country's bestselling and most respected – purpose-built for the modern mountain biker.

The Guidebooks

Each guidebook features up to 28 rides, complete with comprehensive directions, specialist mapping and inspiring photography, all in a pocket-sized, portable format. Written by riders for riders, our guides are designed to maximise ride-ability and are full of useful local area information.

1 SCOTLAND MOUNTAIN BIKING
THE WILD TRAILS

2 SCOTLAND MOUNTAIN BIKING
WILD TRAILS VOL. 2

3 WALES MOUNTAIN BIKING
BEICIO MYNYDD CYMRU

4 LAKE DISTRICT MOUNTAIN BIKING
ESSENTIAL TRAILS

5 YORKSHIRE DALES MOUNTAIN BIKING
THE NORTH DALES

6 YORKSHIRE DALES MOUNTAIN BIKING
THE SOUTH DALES

7 NORTH YORK MOORS MOUNTAIN BIKING
MOORLAND TRAILS

8 WEST YORKSHIRE MOUNTAIN BIKING
SOUTH PENNINE TRAILS

9 PEAK DISTRICT MOUNTAIN BIKING
DARK PEAK TRAILS

10 WHITE PEAK MOUNTAIN BIKING
THE PURE TRAILS

11 COTSWOLDS MOUNTAIN BIKING
20 CLASSIC RIDES

12 SOUTH WEST MOUNTAIN BIKING
QUANTOCKS, EXMOOR, DARTMOOR

13 SOUTH EAST MOUNTAIN BIKING
RIDGEWAY & CHILTERNS

14 SOUTH EAST MOUNTAIN BIKING
NORTH & SOUTH DOWNS

GREAT BRITAIN MOUNTAIN BIKING

A comprehensive area-by-area guide to the best riding in England, Scotland and Wales.

Tom Fenton and Andy McCandlish have compiled everything you need to know about Britain's top riding spots in this ideal companion for planning weekends away.

WITHIN EACH AREA IS:

- a detailed introduction, advice on what kind of riding to expect and when to go;

- at least one featured route – 56 in total – complete with introduction, information box, route directions and **Ordnance Survey** map;

- suggestions for further rides (around 200 rides in total!);

- a detailed information panel with accommodation details, bike shops, trail centres and more.

GREAT BRITAIN
MOUNTAIN BIKING

The best trail riding in England, Scotland and Wales

TOM FENTON & ANDY McCANDLISH

ORDER DIRECT FROM
www.**v-publishing**.co.uk

Eighteen

bikes & custom builds
framebuilding
extensive demo fleet
spares & repairs
clothing & accessories

t   01433 621111
m 07734 653006
e   info@18bikes.co.uk
w www.18bikes.co.uk
a   8 castleton road, hope

find us on: